McDougal Littell

MW00563361

Lab Manual

Earth Science

McDougal Littell
A HOUGHTON MIFFLIN COMPANY
Evanston, Illinois • Boston • Dallas

Acknowledgment

Chapter 4, Earth's Surface

Adaptation of "A Flow Diagram for Teaching Texture-by-Feel Analysis" by Steve J. Thien, for the *Journal of Agronomic Education,* 1979, vol. 8, pp. 54–55. Copyright © 1979 by Steve J. Thien. Reprinted with permission.

ISBN-13: 978-0-618-61540-7   ISBN-10: 0-618-61540-7

5 6 7 8 9-CKI-07 06

EARTH SCIENCE
Lab Manual

Table of Contents

THE CHANGING EARTH

EARTH'S WATERS

SPACE SCIENCE

SECTION | DATASHEET
1.1 | Investigate Geosphere's Layers

How can you model the geosphere's layers?

MATERIALS: apple slice

PROCEDURE

1. As a model of the layers in the geosphere, you will be using a quarter of an apple that your teacher has cut. Note: NEVER eat food in the science classroom.

2. Hold the apple slice and observe it carefully. Compare it with the diagram of the geosphere's layers in your textbook.

3. Draw a diagram of the apple and label it with the names of the layers of the geosphere.

WHAT DO YOU THINK?

What are the four parts of the apple slice?

_____

_____

What major layer of the geosphere does each part of the apple resemble?

_____

_____

CHALLENGE

What other object do you think would make a good model of the geosphere's layers? What model could you build or make yourself?

_____

_____

_____

CHAPTER 1
Views of Earth Today

SECTION | DATASHEET
1.2 | Investigate Map Projections

How do you show the curved Earth on a flat surface?

MATERIALS: top 8 inches of 2-liter bottle, marker pen, walnut-sized piece of clay, poster board, flashlight

PROCEDURE

1 Work in a small group. For a model of the hemisphere, use the top section of a 2-liter plastic bottle that your teacher has cut.

2 Carefully draw three or four latitude lines and six or eight longitude lines on the bottle.

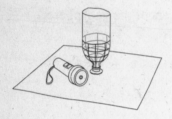

3 Place a piece of clay in the center of a piece of poster board. Press the bottle top into the clay.

4 Shine a flashlight above the center of the model. Trace the lines on the poster board to make your projection.

WHAT DO YOU THINK?

What are the similarities and differences between your model and your projection?

_____

_____

_____

_____

CHALLENGE

Draw a shape on the plastic bottle to represent a landmass. Use the flashlight again to project the hemisphere. How did the shape of the landmass appear when it was projected onto a flat surface?

_____

_____

_____

_____

SECTION | DATASHEET
1.4 | **Investigate Satellite Imaging**

How do satellites send images to Earth?

MATERIALS: graph paper, colored pen or pencil

PROCEDURE

1 Work with a partner. One of you will be the "sensor," and the other will be the "receiving station."

2 The sensor draws the initials of a famous person on a piece of graph paper. The receiving station does NOT see the drawing.

3 The sensor sends the picture to the receiving station. For blank squares, the sensor says "Zero." For filled-in squares, the sensor says "One." Be sure to start at the top row and read left to right, telling the receiving station when a row begins.

4 The receiving station transfers the code to the graph paper. At the end, the receiver has three tries to guess whose initials were sent.

WHAT DO YOU THINK?

What would happen if you accidentally skipped or repeated a row?

_____

_____

If you increased or decreased the number and size of the squares, how would this affect the picture?

_____

_____

_____

CHALLENGE

Use a variety of colors to send other initials or an image. Your code must tell the receiver which code to use for each square.

CHAPTER | CHAPTER INVESTIGATION
1 | Investigate Topographic Maps

OVERVIEW AND PURPOSE
Topographical maps show the shape of the land. In this lab you will use what you have learned about how Earth's three-dimensional surface is represented on maps to

- make a terrain model out of clay
- produce a topographic map of the model

MATERIALS
- half-gallon cardboard juice container
- scissors
- modeling clay
- clear plastic sheet (transparency or sheet protectors)
- cellophane tape
- ruler
- water
- food coloring
- box of spaghetti
- erasable marker pen

Procedure

1. Build a simple landscape about 6–8 cm high from modeling clay. Include a variety of land features. Make sure your model is no taller than the sides of the container.

2. Place your model in the container. Stand a ruler upright inside the container and tape it in place.

3. Lay the clear plastic sheet over the container and tape it on one side like a hinge. Carefully trace the outline of your clay model.

4 Add 2 cm of colored water to the container.

5 Insert spaghetti sticks into the model all around the waterline. Place the sticks about 3 cm apart. Make sure the sticks are straight and are no taller than the sides of the container.

6 Lower the plastic sheet back over the container. Looking straight down on the container, make a dot on the sheet wherever you see a spaghetti stick. Connect the dots to trace the contour line accurately onto your map. See the sample topographic map below as an example of how contour lines may appear.

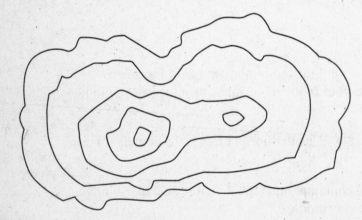

7 Continue adding water, 2 cm at a time. Each time you add water, insert the sticks into the model at the waterline and repeat step 6. Continue until the model landscape is under water. Carefully drain the water when finished.

Observe and Analyze

1. Compare your topographical map with the three-dimensional model. Remember that contour lines connect points of equal elevation. What do widely spaced or tightly spaced contour lines mean? What does a closed circle mean?

_____

_____

_____

2. Make a permanent record of your map to keep in your Science Notebook by carefully tracing the contour lines onto a sheet of white paper. To make reading the map easier, use a different color for the index contour line.

3. What is the contour interval of your model landscape? For example, each 2 centimeters might represent 20 meters on an actual landscape. Record the elevation of your index contour line on your map.

Conclude

1. **Infer** How would you determine the elevation of a point located halfway between two contour lines?

_____

_____

2. **Evaluate** Describe any errors that you may have made in your procedure or any places where errors might have occurred.

_____

_____

_____

3. **Apply** Explain how you would use a topographic map if you were planning a hiking or hiking trip or a cross-country bike race.

_____

_____

_____

_____

CHAPTER | ADDITIONAL INVESTIGATION
1 | # Make a Map by Triangulation

OVERVIEW AND PURPOSE

As you know, a map is a scale drawing of Earth on a flat surface. In this lab, you will use what you've learned about maps to

- construct a simple device called a sextant
- use the sextant to make a scale map

Problem

How can you use a straw and a protractor to make a map?

Procedure

1 Use the pushpin to poke a hole through the center of the straw. Carefully push the ends of the metal paper fastner completely through the hole.

2 Insert the ends of the paper fastener into the hole in the base of the protractor. Secure the straw by spreading the metal ends. Make sure the straw can spin freely. You have made a sighting device called a *sextant*.

MATERIALS
- small, thin, metal paper fastener
- pushpin
- masking tape
- meter stick
- sharp pencil
- plastic protractor with a small hole in its base
- large plastic straw about 20 cm long
- 2 wooden stakes
- large sheet of plain paper, about 1 m²

TIME
45 minutes

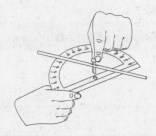

3 Take your sextant and other materials outdoors. Work with one or two other students to select an area to map. The area that you are going to map should include signposts, trees, a flagpole, playground equipment, or other similar objects.

4 Use the meter stick to figure out which area you will map. The area should be 10 m × 10 m or smaller.

5 Along one edge of your area, use the string to mark off a baseline. First, use the hammer to push the wooden stakes in the ground. Put one stake at each end of the baseline, as shown in the figure. Make sure that the wooden stakes are the same height above the ground.

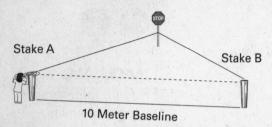

Stake A

Stake B

10 Meter Baseline

6 Use the meter stick to measure the length of your baseline. Record this measurement in Data Table 1.1.

7 Use the masking tape to secure the sextant to wooden Stake A. The base of the sextant must be parallel to your baseline.

8 Sight an object in your map area through the straw. Record the object and the angle shown on the protractor in the data table.

9 Now secure the sextant to Stake B. Repeat steps 7 and 8, sighting the same object from Stake B. Record the angle shown on the sextant in the third column of the data table.

10 Repeat steps 7 through 9 for many of the large objects in your map area.

DATA TABLE 1.1: ANGLES SHOWN ON SEXTANT		
Object Sighted	**Angle from Stake A**	**Angle from Stake B**

11 Use the meter stick to measure the actual distances between pairs of objects sighted. Record the objects and measurements in Data Table 1.2.

12 Collect all of your materials and take them back inside. Remove the straw from the protractor.

13 Use a map scale of 1 cm to 1 m to draw your baseline along the bottom edge of the large sheet of plain paper. Mark the end of each baseline with a small dot. Label these points "Stake A" and "Stake B," as shown in the figure. Make sure your map includes a map scale.

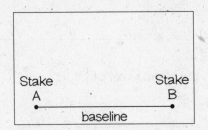

14 Place your protractor on the point labeled Stake A. Use a ruler and a pencil to draw the angle for the first object sighted from Stake A. Place your protractor on the point labeled Stake B. Use the ruler to draw the angle for the first object sighted from Stake B. The point where the lines meet is the location of the object. Label this point with the name of the object, such as "flagpole." Erase the lines you drew.

15 Repeat step 14 for all of the objects sighted.

16 Measure and record in Data Table 1.2 the map distances between pairs of objects.

DATA TABLE 1.2: ACTUAL DISTANCE AND MAP DISTANCE		
Object to Object	**Actual Distance (m)**	**Map Distance (cm)**
Stake to stake (baseline)		

Observe and Analyze

1. Model What is the purpose of your baseline?

_____

_____

_____

2. **Compare** Compare your map distances for all of the objects sighted with the actual distances. Explain any large differences.

_____

_____

_____

3. **Explain** Could you have mapped an area twice the size on the same sheet of paper? Explain.

_____

_____

_____

4. **Explain** The mapping method you used in this investigation is called *triangulation*. Why do you think it is called that name?

_____

_____

_____

Conclude

1. **Identify limits** How close were the actual distances to your map distances? How might you improve the accuracy of your map?

_____

_____

_____

2. **Apply** How could you use a sextant to map objects behind a baseline? What would your new sextant look like?

_____

_____

_____

3. **Infer** If you had mapped a smaller area, would your map have been more accurate or less accurate? Explain why.

_____

_____

_____

2.1 | Investigate Crystal Shape

How do crystals differ in shape?

MATERIALS: tablespoon, 2 mixing cups, 2 stirring rods, 1 tablespoon table salt,
1 tablespoon Epsom salts, 60 mL water, 2 pie plates, 2 sheets black paper, scissors

PROCEDURE

1 Cut sheets of paper so that they fit inside the pie plates. Place one sheet in each pie plate.

2 Add the table salt to 30 mL of water in the cup. Stir the water until the salt has dissolved.

3 Pour enough salt solution into one of the pie plates to completely cover the paper with a small film of liquid. Be careful not to pour into the plate any undissolved salt that may be in the bottom of the cup.

4 Repeat steps 2 and 3 with the Epsom salts. Let the plates dry overnight.

WHAT DO YOU THINK?

Compare and describe the shapes of the crystals.

_____

_____

What do you think accounts for any differences you observe?

_____

_____

CHALLENGE

Why are the shapes of the crystals the same as or different from the shapes in the materials you started with?

_____

_____

_____

CHAPTER 2
Minerals

SECTION | DATASHEET
2.2 | # Investigate Hardness of Minerals

How hard are some common minerals?

MATERIALS: samples of 5 minerals, copper penny, steel file

PROCEDURE

1 Try to scratch each mineral with your fingernail, the penny, and the steel file. Record your results below.

2 Use your results to assign a hardness range in the Mohs scale to each sample.

Mohs Scale

1	2	3	4	5	6	7	8	9	10
Talc	Gypsum	Calcite	Fluorite	Apatite	Feldspar	Quartz	Topaz	Corundum	Diamond

3 In the last column of the chart, rank the minerals from hardest to softest.

	Mineral	Fingernail	Penny	Steel File	Hardness Range	Rank
1						
2						
3						
4						
5						

WHAT DO YOU THINK?

If two minerals have the same hardness range according to your tests, how could you tell which is harder?

_____

CHALLENGE

If you had a mineral that could not be scratched by the steel file, what might you test it with to estimate its hardness?

_____

SECTION | DATASHEET
2.3 | Investigate Mining

What are the benefits and costs of mining ores?

MATERIALS: 1 pound wild-birdseed mix with sunflower seeds, shallow pan, 2 small red beads, 4 small green beads, 8 small blue beads, 3 medium yellow beads

PROCEDURE

1 Put the wild-birdseed into a pan. Add the beads to the birdseed and mix well.

2 Search through the seeds and separate the beads and sunflower seeds, placing each kind in a different pile. Take no more than 3 minutes.

3 Assign a value to each of the beads and seeds: red bead, $5; green bead, $4; blue bead, $3; and sunflower seeds, $2. Count the value of your beads and seeds. For every yellow bead, subtract $100, which represents the cost of restoring the land after mining.

WHAT DO YOU THINK?

How does the difficulty of finding the red beads relate to the difficulty of finding the most valuable ores?

_____

_____

How does the total value of the blue beads and the sunflower seeds compare to the total value of the red and green beads? What can you conclude about deciding which materials to mine?

_____

_____

CHALLENGE

The sunflower seeds and the red, green, and blue beads could represent minerals that contain copper, gold, iron, and silver. Which bead or seed is most likely to represent which mineral? Explain your choices.

_____

_____

CHAPTER 2 | DATASHEET

Mineral Identification Key

In this table, minerals are arranged in order of increasing hardness. The most useful properties for identification are printed in *italic* type. The colors listed are the most common for each mineral.

Name	Hardness	Color	Streak	Cleavage	Remarks
Talc	*1*	Apple-green, gray, white	White	Perfect in one direction	Nonmetallic (pearly to greasy) luster. Nonelastic flakes, *greasy feel.* Sp. gr. 2.7 to 2.8.
Graphite	1–2	*Dark gray to black*	Grayish black	*Perfect in one direction*	Metallic or nonmetallic (earthy) luster. *Greasy feel, marks paper.* This is the "lead" in a pencil (mixed with clay). Sp. gr. 2.2.
Gypsum	*2*	Colorless, white, gray, yellowish, reddish	White	*Perfect in one direction*	Nonmetallic (glassy to silky) luster. *Can be scratched easily by a fingernail.* Sp. gr. 2.3.
Halite	2–2.5	Colorless, white	White	*Perfect, three directions, at 90° angles*	Nonmetallic (glassy) luster. *Salty taste.* Sp. gr. 2.2.
Muscovite mica	2–2.5	Colorless in thin films; silvery, yellowish, and greenish in thicker pieces	*White*	Perfect in one direction	Nonmetallic (glassy to pearly) luster. *Thin elastic films peel off readily.* Sp. gr. 2.8 to 2.9.
Galena	2.5	*Lead gray*	Lead gray	*Perfect, three directions, at 90° angles*	*Metallic luster.* Occurs as crystals and masses. *Dense.* Sp. gr. 7.4 to 7.6.
Biotite mica	2.5–3	Black, brown, dark green	White	*Perfect in one direction*	Nonmetallic (glassy) luster. *Thin elastic films peel off easily.* Sp. gr. 2.8 to 3.2.
Copper	2.5–3	*Copper red*	Copper	None	*Metallic luster on fresh surface. Dense.* Sp. gr. 8.9.
Calcite	*3*	White, colorless	White	*Perfect, three directions, not at 90° angles*	Nonmetallic (glassy to dull) luster. *Fizzes in dilute hydrochloric acid.* Sp. gr. 2.7.
Chalcopyrite	3.5–4	*Golden yellow*	Greenish black	Poor in one direction	Metallic luster. *Hardness distinguishes from pyrite.* Sp. gr. 4.1 to 4.3.
Dolomite	3.5–4	Pinkish, colorless, white	White	*Perfect, three directions, not at 90° angles*	Nonmetallic luster. *Scratched surface fizzes in dilute hydrochloric acid. Cleavage surfaces curved.* Sp. gr. 2.8 to 2.9.

Name	Hardness	Color	Streak	Cleavage	Remarks
Sphalerite	3.5–4	Yellow, brown, black	Yellow to light brown	Perfect, six directions	Nonmetallic (brilliant to resinous) luster. Sp. gr. 3.9 to 4.1.
Fluorite	4	Varies	White	Perfect, four directions	Nonmetallic (glassy) luster. In cubes or octahedrons as crystals. Sp. gr. 3.2.
Apatite	5	Green, brown	White	Poor in one direction	Nonmetallic (glassy) luster. Sp. gr. 3.1 to 3.2.
Augite	5–6	Dark green to black	Greenish	Two directions nearly at 90°	Nonmetallic (glassy) luster. Stubby four- or eight-sided crystals. Common type of pyroxene. Sp. gr. 3.2 to 3.4.
Hematite	5–6 (may appear softer)	Reddish-brown, gray, black	Reddish	None	Metallic or nonmetallic (earthy) luster. Dense. Sp. gr. 5.3.
Hornblende	5–6	Dark green to black	Brown to gray	Perfect, two directions at angles of 56° and 124°	Nonmetallic (glassy to silky) luster. Common type of amphibole. Long, slender, six-sided crystals. Sp. gr. 3.0 to 3.4.
Magnetite	5.5–6.5	Black	Black	None	Metallic luster. Occurs as eight-sided crystals and granular masses. Magnetic. Dense. Sp. gr. 5.2.
Feldspar (Orthoclase)	6	Salmon pink, red, white, light gray	White	Good, two directions, 90° intersection	Nonmetallic (glassy) luster. Hardness, color, and cleavage taken together are diagnostic. Sp. gr. 2.6.
Feldspar (Plagioclase)	6	White to light gray, can be salmon pink	White	Good, two directions, about 90°	Nonmetallic (glassy or pearly) luster. If striations are visible, they are diagnostic. Sp. gr. 2.6 to 2.8.
Pyrite	6–6.5	Brass yellow	Greenish black	None	Metallic luster. Cubic crystals and granular masses. Dense. Sp. gr. 5.0 to 5.1.
Olivine	6.5–7	Yellowish, greenish	White	None	Nonmetallic (glassy) luster. Granular. Sp. gr. 3.3 to 4.4.
Quartz	7	Colorless, white; varies	White	None	Nonmetallic (glassy) luster. Conchoidal fracture. Six-sided crystals common. Many varieties. Sp. gr. 2.6.
Topaz	8	Varies	White	Perfect in one direction	Nonmetallic (brilliant to glassy) luster. Crystals commonly striated length-wise. Sp. gr. 3.4 to 3.6.
Corundum	9	Brown, pink, blue	White	None, parting resembles cleavage	Nonmetallic (glassy to brilliant) luster. Barrel-shaped, six-sided crystals with flat ends. Sp. gr. 4.0.

CHAPTER 2
Minerals

Sp. gr. = specific gravity

CHAPTER | DATASHEET
2 | **Mohs Scale**

Mohs Scale
1 Talc
2 Gypsum
3 Calcite
4 Fluorite
5 Apatite
6 Feldspar
7 Quartz
8 Topaz
9 Corundum
10 Diamond

CHAPTER
2 | CHAPTER INVESTIGATION
Mineral Identification

OVERVIEW AND PURPOSE

In this activity, you will observe and perform tests on minerals. Then you will compare your observations with a mineral identification key.

Procedure

1 You will examine and identify five minerals. Get a numbered mineral sample from the mineral set. Record the number of your sample in your data table below.

MATERIALS
- numbered mineral samples
- hand lens
- streak plate
- copper penny
- steel file
- magnet
- dilute hydrochloric acid
- eyedropper
- Mohs scale
- Mineral Identification Key

CHAPTER 2
Minerals

Property	Sample Number				
	1	2	3	4	5
Color					
Luster					
Cleavage					
Fracture					
Streak					
Hardness					
Special Tests					
Magnetic					
Acid Test					
Name of Mineral					

TABLE 1. MINERAL PROPERTIES

❷ First, observe the sample. Note the color and the luster of the sample. Write these observations in your data table. In the row marked "Luster," write *metallic* if the mineral appears shiny like metal. Write *non-metallic* if the sample does not look like metal. For example, it may look glassy, pearly, or dull.

❸ Observe the sample through the hand lens. Look to see any signs of how the crystals in the mineral broke. If it appears that the crystal has broken along straight lines, put a check in the row marked "Cleavage." If it appears that the sample has fractured, put a check in that row on your data table.

❹ CAUTION: Keep the streak plate on your desktop or table while you are doing the streak test. A broken streak plate can cause serious cuts. Rub the mineral sample across the streak plate. If the sample doesn't leave a mark, the sample is harder than the streak plate. Write *No* in the row labeled "Streak." If the sample does leave a mark on the streak plate, write the color of the streak in that row.

❺ Test each of the samples for hardness according to the Mohs hardness scale. Try to scratch the sample with each of these items in order: your fingernail, a copper penny, and a steel file. Using the Mohs scale, find the hardness number for the object that first scratches the sample. Write in the data table that the mineral's hardness value is between that of the hardest item that did not scratch the sample and that of the item that did scratch it.

TABLE 2. MOHS HARDNESS SCALE		
Talc	1	Scratched by a fingernail
Gypsum	2	
Calcite	3	Scratched by a copper coin
Fluorite	4	Scratched by a knife blade or window glass
Apatite	5	
Feldspar	6	Scratches a knife blade or window glass
Quartz	7	
Topaz	8	
Corundum	9	
Diamond	10	Scratches all common materials

6 Test each of the samples with the magnet. If the sample is attracted to the magnet, put a checkmark in the row marked "Magnetic."

7 Repeat steps 1 through 6 for each of the numbered samples.

Observe and Analyze

1. **Interpret Data** Use the Mineral Identification Key and the information in your data table to identify your samples. Write the names of the minerals on your data table.

2. **Collect Data** CAUTION: Before doing the acid test, put on your safety glasses, protective gloves, and lab apron. Acids can cause burns. If you identified one of the samples as a carbonate mineral, such as calcite, you can check your identification with the acid test. Use the eyedropper to put a few drops of dilute hydrochloric acid on the mineral. If the acid bubbles, the sample is a carbonate.

Conclude

1. **Compare and Contrast** How are the minerals calcite and halite alike? Which property can you use to test whether a sample is calcite or halite?

_____
_____
_____
_____

2. **Interpret** Look at the results on your data table. Name any minerals that you could identify on the basis of a single property.

_____
_____
_____
_____

3. **Apply** Examine a piece of granite rock. On the basis of your examination of granite and your observations of the samples, try to determine what the light-colored, translucent mineral in the granite is and what the flaky, darker mineral is.

_____
_____
_____
_____

CHAPTER 2
Minerals

CHAPTER **2** | ADDITIONAL INVESTIGATION
Stalagmites and Stalactites

OVERVIEW AND PURPOSE
As you know, minerals form as the result of natural processes. Minerals develop when the atoms of one or more elements join and crystals begin to grow. In this lab, you will use what you have learned about minerals to

- demonstrate how minerals form as the result of evaporation
- model the formation of stalagmites and stalactites

Problem
How can you demonstrate that some minerals form when water evaporates?

Hypothesize
Read the procedure. Use what you know about minerals to form a hypothesis. Explain how you will model the way in which minerals form on the ceilings and floors of caves.

_____

_____

_____

MATERIALS
- yarn
- glue
- scissors
- shoe box
- metric ruler
- transparent tape
- 800-mL beaker
- Epsom salts
- hot tap water
- measuring cup
- stirring rod
- aluminum foil
- fine-lined permanent marker
- metal knitting needle (about 0.4 cm in diameter)
- 2–3 plastic drinking cups whose top diameters are slightly smaller than the width of the long side of the shoe box

TIME
45 minutes

CHAPTER 2
Minerals

Procedure

1 Turn the shoe box on its side so that it rests on one of its long sides. Line this long side with aluminum foil. Use tape to hold the foil in place.

2 Use the top of one of the plastic cups to trace two or three circles on the top of the other long side of the box, as shown. Trace only the number of circles that will fit without overlapping.

3 Carefully use the knitting needle to punch four holes around the circumference of each circle. Make the holes at the 12 o'clock, 3 o'clock, 6 o'clock, and 9 o'clock positions of a clock face.

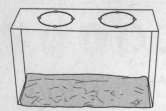

4 Glue the bottoms of the cups into the circles. Do not cover any of the holes. Wait for the glue to dry completely.

5 Cut a piece of yarn about 50 cm long. Put one end of this piece of yarn into one of the cups. Make sure the yarn touches the bottom of the cup. Gently pull the yarn through one of the holes surrounding this cup. Make sure the yarn still touches the bottom of the cup. Trim the yarn so that only about 10 cm of it hangs into the box.

 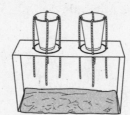

6 Repeat step 5 for all of the other holes surrounding the cups. Vary the length of the yarn hanging in the box from about 5 cm to about 10 cm. Make sure the yarn does not touch the outside of the cups.

7 Carefully pour 4 cups of hot tap water into the beaker.

8 Add 5 cups of Epsom salts to the hot water and stir until all of the salt dissolves.

9 Carefully pour the salt solution into the cups until the cups are about 7/8 full.

10 Observe your box every day for the next week. Get your teacher's approval to make and add more salt solution as the water evaporates.

CHAPTER 2
Minerals

11 Below, draw a side view of your "cave" two or three days after you made it. Draw the same view after 5 days. Draw the "cave" again after a week or so.

"Cave" After 2 or 3 Days	"Cave" After 5 Days	"Cave" After 7 or More Days

Observe and Analyze

1. **Explain** Why was it helpful to add such large amounts of Epsom salts to the hot tap water?

_____

_____

_____

_____

2. **Explain** Why was it important that the yarn not touch the outsides of the cups?

_____

_____

_____

_____

3. **Observe** Stalactites are structures that hang from the ceilings of a cave. Explain how your stalactites formed.

_____

_____

_____

_____

4. **Observe** Stalagmites are structures that "grow" upward from a cave's floor. Explain how your stalagmites formed.

_____

_____

_____

_____

5. **Explain** Which structures formed first in your model—the stalactites or the stalagmites? Explain why.

_____

_____

_____

6. **Compare** Observe the shapes of your stalactites and stalagmites. How are they the same? How do they differ?

_____

_____

_____

Conclude

1. **Predict** Predict how you could increase the rate of mineral formation in this investigation.

_____

_____

_____

2. **Apply** How could you increase the size of the mineral crystals that form in the cave?

_____

_____

_____

3. **Draw Conclusions** In this investigation, you added the minerals (Epsom salts) to the water to form the solution. Where do the dissolved minerals that form structures in an actual cave come from?

_____

_____

_____

SECTION | DATASHEET
3.1 | Investigate Classification of Rocks

How can rocks be classified?

MATERIALS 5 rock samples

PROCEDURE

1 Examine the rock samples. Look at their physical characteristics.

2 Make a list on a separate sheet of paper of the differences in the physical characteristics of the rocks.

3 Use your list to decide which characteristics of the rocks are most important in classifying the rocks into different types. Write the five most important characteristics in the spaces below the *Characteristics* heading. Complete the chart showing the different rock characteristics. Then classify the rocks into types by using the chart.

CHARACTERISTICS					
Rock					
1					
2					
3					
4					
5					

WHAT DO YOU THINK?

Which physical characteristic is most helpful in classifying the rocks?

_____

Which physical characteristic is least helpful in classifying the rocks?

_____

CHALLENGE

Is it possible to classify rocks only by the characteristics you can see?

_____

_____

SECTION | DATASHEET
3.2 | Mineral Crystal Diagrams

Match each rock diagram with the graph that shows how quickly it cooled.

Igneous
Rock A

Description _____
_____
_____

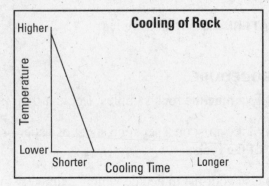

1. _____

Description _____
_____
_____

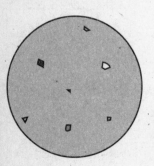

Igneous
Rock B

Description _____
_____
_____

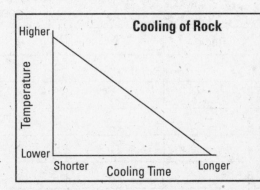

2. _____

Description _____
_____
_____

Igneous
Rock C

Description _____
_____
_____

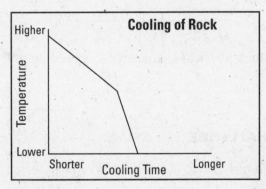

3. _____

Description _____
_____
_____

CHAPTER 3
Rocks

SECTION
3.2 | DATASHEET
Investigate Crystal Size

How does cooling time affect crystal size?

MATERIALS Mineral Crystal Diagrams datasheet

PROCEDURE

❶ Look at the Mineral Crystal Diagrams datasheet.

❷ Describe your observations of the crystals in each of the igneous-rock diagrams A–C on the lines provided.

❸ Describe what is shown in each of graphs 1–3 on the lines provided.

❹ Match each igneous-rock diagram with its corresponding diagram.

❺ On the back of the paper, explain why you matched each crystal diagram with a particular graph.

WHAT DO YOU THINK?

Which diagram shows an intrusive igneous rock, such as gabbro?

_____

_____

Where do you think the rock shown in diagram B formed? Explain your answer.

_____

_____

_____

CHALLENGE

Write a hypothesis to explain why the rock shown in diagram C might be found at a shallow depth in Earth's crust.

_____

_____

_____

CHAPTER 3
Rocks

SECTION | DATASHEET
3.3 | Investigate Rock Layers

How do sedimentary rocks form in layers?

MATERIALS 1 paper cup, 3 mixing cups, 6 tbs plaster of Paris, 3 tbs water, 4 tbs gravel, 2 tbs sand, 3 drops of food coloring

PROCEDURE

1. Prepare the plaster of Paris by mixing it with the water.

2. Mix 2 tablespoons of the gravel or pebbles with 2 tablespoons of the plaster of Paris and pour the mixture into the paper cup.

3. Mix the sand with 2 tablespoons of the plaster of Paris and the food coloring. Add the mixture to the paper cup on top of the gravel mixture.

4. Mix the rest of the gravel with the rest of the plaster of Paris. Add the mixture to the paper cup, on top of the sand mixture.

5. After the mixture hardens for about 5 minutes, tear apart the paper cup and observe the layers.

WHAT DO YOU THINK?

How is the procedure you used to make your model similar to the way sedimentary rock forms?

_____

_____

Describe how similar layers of real rock could form.

_____

_____

_____

_____

CHALLENGE

How would you create a model to show the formation of fossil-rich limestone?

_____

_____

CHAPTER 3
Rocks

SECTION
DATASHEET
3.4 | Investigate Metamorphic Changes

How can pressure and temperature change a solid?

MATERIALS 3 candles of different colors, vegetable peeler

PROCEDURE

① Use a vegetable peeler to make a handful of wax shavings of three colors. Mix the shavings.

② Use your hands to warm the shavings, and then squeeze them into a wafer.

WHAT DO YOU THINK?

Describe what happened to the wax shavings.

_____

_____

How do the changes you observed resemble metamorphic changes in rocks?

_____

_____

_____

CHALLENGE

What changes that occur in metamorphic rocks were you unable to model in this experiment?

_____

_____

CHAPTER 3
Rocks

CHAPTER | DATASHEET
3 | Rock Classification Key

Match each rock diagram with the graph that shows how quickly it cooled.

1. **Look at the composition of your rock. Is the rock made up of visible particles (for example, mineral crystals or sand)?**

   a. Some or all of the particles are visible. [go to step 3]

   b. The rock does not contain any visible particles. [go to step 2]

2. **Look at the texture of your rock. Is the rock glassy, porous (sponge-like), or completely solid?**

   a. The rock is glassy or porous. [the rock is igneous]

   b. The rock is completely solid. [go to step 5]

3. **Determine the type of particles that make up the rock.**

   a. The rock has visible mineral crystals. [go to step 4]

   b. The rock is made up of individual particles (such as sand or pebbles) that are cemented together. [the rock is sedimentary]

4. **Determine if the mineral crystals of the rock tend to line up or form bands.**

   a. The mineral crystals are not lined up in any particular direction. [go to step 7]

   b. The mineral crystals tend to line up or to form bands. [the rock is metamorphic]

5. **Determine if the rock is made up of layers or if it tends to break into layers.**

   a. The rock has no layers and does not break into layers. [the rock is igneous]

   b. The rock has layers or tends to break into layers. [go to step 6]

6. **Determine how shiny the rock is.**

   a. The rock is not shiny. [the rock is sedimentary]

   b. The rock is somewhat to quite shiny. [the rock is metamorphic]

7. **Determine if the rock is made up of one or more types of mineral crystals.**

   a. All the crystals appear to be of the same mineral. [the rock is metamorphic]

   b. The crystals are of two or more types of minerals. [the rock is igneous]

CHAPTER

3

CHAPTER INVESTIGATION

Rock Classification

OVERVIEW AND PURPOSE

In this activity, you will examine rock samples and refer to a
rock classification key. You will classify each sample as igneous,
sedimentary, or metamorphic.

MATERIALS
• magnifying lens
• 6–8 rock samples
• Rock Classification Key

Procedure

1 Get a numbered rock sample. Record its number in the table below.

TABLE 1		
Sample Number	**Description of Its Visible Properties**	**Rock Class**

CHAPTER 3
Rocks

2 Observe the sample as a whole. Then closely examine it with the hand lens. Record in your table all visual properties of the sample. For example, include properties such as mineral or sediment size, layering, or banding.

3 Look at the classification key. Each item in the key consists of paired statements. Start with item 1 of the key. Choose the statement that best describes the rock you are examining. Look at the end of the statement and then go to the item number indicated.

4 Examine the rock sample again and choose the statement that best describes the rock.

5 Continue to work through the key until your choices lead you to a classification that fits your rock. Repeat steps 1–4 for each of the numbered samples.

Observe and Analyze

1. **Interpret** Referring to the Rock Classification Key and the observations you recorded, write the type of each rock in your data table.

2. **Identify Limits** What problems, if any, did you experience in applying the key? Which samples did not seem to fit easily into a category? How could you improve the key?

_____

_____

_____

_____

Conclude

1. **Compare and Contrast** How are igneous and metamorphic rocks similar? How can you tell them apart?

_____

_____

_____

2. **Analyze** Examine a sample of sedimentary rock in which visible particles are cemented together. In addition to sight, what other sense could help you classify the rock sample? Explain your answer.

_____

_____

3. **Apply** What have you learned from this investigation that would help you make a classification key that someone else could follow? How would you make a key to classify a music collection? Write two pairs of numbered statements that would start the classification process.

_____

_____

_____

_____

_____

CHAPTER 3
Rocks

CHAPTER
3

ADDITIONAL INVESTIGATION

Modeling Rock Formation

OVERVIEW AND PURPOSE

As you know, different rocks form in different ways. In this investigation, you will use what you've learned about rocks to

- model some of the ways in which rocks form
- identify the rocks represented by your models

Problem

How can you model some of the processes that form rocks?

Procedure

1. Put on your safety goggles. Leave them on until you have *completely* finished this investigation.

2. Cut the candles into small pieces. Remove the wicks. Put half of the pieces into one of the small pans. Put the rest of the pieces into the other pan. Put the pans on the hot plate.

3. Once you have your teacher's permission to use the hot plate, turn it on high. **CAUTION:** Be careful when using any heat source.

4. When the wax has completely melted, turn off the hot plate. Use the tongs to remove one of the pans. Put the pan aside. Put the irregularly shaped craft beads into this pan.

5. Use the tongs to remove the other pan from the hot plate. Turn the hot plate off. Carefully and slowly pour the melted wax into the beaker of cold water. Don't let the melted wax touch the sides of the beaker.

6. After about 10 minutes, observe the wax in both containers. Record your observations in the data table.

7. Warm the modeling clay with your hands. Roll the clay into a large ball. Place the small, long craft beads into the ball. Make sure the craft beads are spread throughout the clay.

8. Put the ball of clay between two pieces of waxed paper. Use the rolling pin to flatten the clay into a rectangle.

9. Remove the clay from the waxed paper. Study the clay. Record your observations in the data table.

10. Put the salt into one of the pans. Add just enough water to dissolve the salt while stirring with a craft stick. Put the pan back on the hot plate.

MATERIALS
- 20 small thin candles
- plastic knife
- 3 small aluminum pans
- hot plate
- tongs
- 10 small plastic craft beads—all different shapes
- 400 mL beaker half full of cold tap water
- modeling clay (about 250 g)
- 20 small plastic craft beads—long
- waxed paper
- rolling pin
- salt (about 100 g)
- 2 craft sticks
- sand grains (about 75 g)
- pea gravel (about 25 g)
- spoon
- white glue
- 2 small paper cups

TIME: 45 minutes

CHAPTER 3
Rocks

⓫ Repeat step 3.

⓬ Heat until all the water has evaporated. Use the tongs to remove the pan, and put it aside. Turn the hot plate off.

⓭ Put the sand grains, the pea gravel, and two spoons of white glue into the other small paper cup. Mix the materials with a craft stick.

⓮ After the glue has completely dried, tear the cup off of the hardened mixture. Observe the mixture and record your observations in the data table.

DATA TABLE 3.1: MODELING ROCK-FORMING PROCESSES	
Process	Observations
melting candle wax	
flattening a ball of clay	
Recrystallizing salt	
mixing sand, gravel, and glue	

Observe and Analyze

1. **Model** What type of "rock" did you make in steps 2–5?

   _____

2. **Explain** What rock cycle processes did you model in steps 2–5?

   _____

   _____

   _____

3. **Model** What type of "rock" did you make in steps 7–9?

   _____

4. **Explain** What rock cycle processes did you model in steps 7–9?

   _____

   _____

   _____

5. **Model** What type of "rocks" did you make in steps 10–13?

   _____

6. **Explain** What rock cycle processes did you model in steps 10–13?

   _____

   _____

   _____

CHAPTER 3
Rocks

Conclude

1. **Apply** What similarities exist between the processes that form igneous and metamorphic rocks? What is the major difference in how these two types of rocks form?

_____

_____

_____

2. **Apply** How do the processes that form sedimentary rocks differ from those that result in igneous and metamorphic rocks?

_____

_____

_____

3. **Identify Limits** How was this investigation similar to the formation of actual rocks? How was it different?

_____

_____

_____

4. **Synthesize** Use what you know about rocks to describe how a sedimentary rock can form from a deeply buried igneous rock.

_____

_____

_____

CHAPTER 3
Rocks

4.1 Investigate Chemical Weathering

What is necessary for rust to form?

MATERIALS: steel wool, 3 cups, water

PROCEDURE

1 Place a piece of steel wool in a cup filled to the top with water. Place a second piece of steel wool in a cup with a small amount of water. The water should touch but not cover the steel wool. Place a third piece in a cup with no water.

2 Allow the three cups to sit overnight. Observe the appearance of the steel wool in each container the next day.

WHAT DO YOU THINK?

1. What happened to the steel wool in each cup?

   _____

   _____

   _____

2. Judging by the appearance of the pieces of steel wool, what do you think is necessary for rusting to occur?

   _____

   _____

CHALLENGE

Tear the steel wool that rusted most apart and compare the appearances of the inside and the outside. Why might the inside and the outside look different?

_____

_____

_____

CHAPTER 4
Weathering and Soil Formation

SECTION | DATASHEET
4.3 | Apple Chart

Use the chart below as you complete the activity. The first column contains a description of each step. The second column describes what each step represents. In the third column, draw a picture of what your apple looks like at each step.

Description of step	What does it represent?	Drawing
1. Cut the apple into quarters and set aside three of the quarters.	• The three quarters you set aside represent the amount of Earth that is covered by the ocean. • The one quarter left over represents all the land on Earth that is above the ocean.	
2. Cut the one quarter that represents Earth's land in half. Set aside one of these pieces.	• The piece you set aside represents land too hot, cold, steep, wet, dry or otherwise uninhabitable by people. • The other piece represents the land where people live.	
3. Cut the piece that represents the land where people live into four sections. Set aside three sections.	• The three pieces you set aside represent land that cannot support food crops.	
4. Peel the skin off of the remaining one section.	• The peel represents the amount of land on Earth with fertile soil, capable of supporting agriculture. • It is this tiny portion of land that humans rely on for almost all food production.	

CHAPTER 4
Weathering and Soil Formation

SECTION 4.3 | DATASHEET
Investigate Soil Conservation

How can you model Earth's soil with an apple?

MATERIALS: Apple Chart, apple, plastic knife

PROCEDURE

1 Fill in a row of the Apple Chart as you complete each step.

2 Cut the apple into quarters. Set aside three of the quarters.

3 Cut the remaining quarter in half. Set aside one of these pieces.

4 Cut the remaining piece from step 3 into four pieces. Set aside three of them.

5 Peel the skin off the remaining piece from step 4.

WHAT DO YOU THINK?

1. How does the amount of fertile soil on Earth compare with what you expected?

_____

_____

2. Do you think that the amount of fertile soil on Earth is increasing or decreasing? Explain your answer.

_____

_____

_____

CHALLENGE

Invent a method of soil conservation other than the ones you have read about. How would your method help keep soil in place?

_____

_____

_____

_____

CHAPTER 4
Weathering and Soil Formation

CHAPTER
4 | DATASHEET
Texture Flow Chart

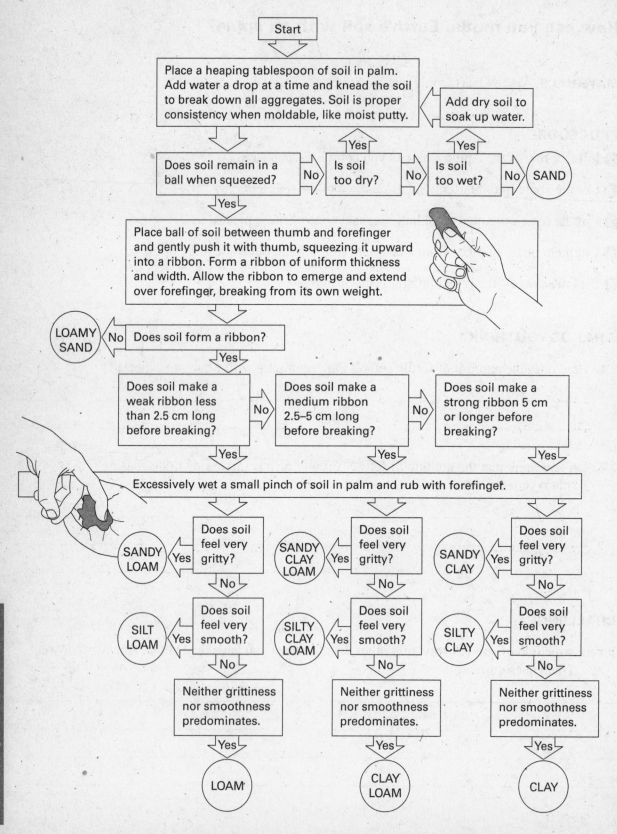

Start

↓

Place a heaping tablespoon of soil in palm. Add water a drop at a time and knead the soil to break down all aggregates. Soil is proper consistency when moldable, like moist putty. ← Add dry soil to soak up water.

Does soil remain in a ball when squeezed? —No→ Is soil too dry? —Yes↑ —No→ Is soil too wet? —Yes↑ —No→ SAND

↓Yes

Place ball of soil between thumb and forefinger and gently push it with thumb, squeezing it upward into a ribbon. Form a ribbon of uniform thickness and width. Allow the ribbon to emerge and extend over forefinger, breaking from its own weight.

↓

LOAMY SAND ←No— Does soil form a ribbon?

↓Yes

Does soil make a weak ribbon less than 2.5 cm long before breaking? —No→ Does soil make a medium ribbon 2.5–5 cm long before breaking? —No→ Does soil make a strong ribbon 5 cm or longer before breaking?

↓Yes ↓Yes ↓Yes

Excessively wet a small pinch of soil in palm and rub with forefinger.

↓ ↓ ↓

SANDY LOAM ←Yes— Does soil feel very gritty?
SANDY CLAY LOAM ←Yes— Does soil feel very gritty?
SANDY CLAY ←Yes— Does soil feel very gritty?

↓No ↓No ↓No

SILT LOAM ←Yes— Does soil feel very smooth?
SILTY CLAY LOAM ←Yes— Does soil feel very smooth?
SILTY CLAY ←Yes— Does soil feel very smooth?

↓No ↓No ↓No

Neither grittiness nor smoothness predominates.
Neither grittiness nor smoothness predominates.
Neither grittiness nor smoothness predominates.

↓Yes ↓Yes ↓Yes

LOAM
CLAY LOAM
CLAY

CHAPTER 4
Weathering and Soil Formation

CHAPTER

CHAPTER INVESTIGATION

4 | Testing Soil

OVERVIEW AND PURPOSE

Soil is necessary for life. Whether a soil is suitable for farming
or construction, and whether it absorbs water when it rains,
depends on the particular properties of that soil. In this
investigation you will

- test a soil sample to measure several soil properties
- identify the properties of your soil sample

Procedure

PORE-SPACE TEST

MATERIALS
- dried soil sample
- 250-mL graduated
  cylinder
- 1-qt jar with lid
- water
- 2-L plastic bottle
- scissors
- window screening
- rubber band
- pH test strips
- clock with second
  hand

1 Measure 200 mL of the dried soil sample in a graduated cylinder. Pour it into
the jar.

2 Rinse the graduated cylinder, then fill it with 200 mL of water. Slowly pour the
water into the jar until the soil is so soaked that any additional water would pool
on top.

3 Record the amount of water remaining in the graduated cylinder. Then determine
by subtraction the amount you added to the soil sample. Record this number in
Table 1.

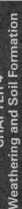
CHAPTER 4
Weathering and Soil Formation

TABLE 1. SOIL PROPERTIES CHART		
Property	**Result**	**Notes and Calculations**
Pore space	_____mL water added	
pH	before: pH = _____ after: pH = _____	
Drainage	_____ seconds	
Particle type	height of sand = _____cm height of silt = _____cm height of clay = _____cm total height = _____cm	

4 Discard the wet soil according to your teacher's instructions, and rinse the jar.

pH TEST AND DRAINAGE TEST

5 Cut off the top of a plastic bottle and use a rubber band to attach a piece of window screening over its mouth. Place the bottle top, mouth down, into the jar.

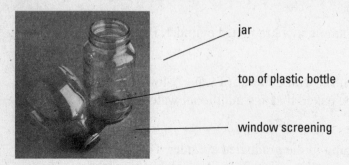

jar

top of plastic bottle

window screening

6 Use the graduated cylinder to measure 200 mL of soil. Pour the soil into the inverted bottle top.

7 Rinse the graduated cylinder, and fill it with 100 mL of water. Test the water's pH, using a pH test strip. Record the result in the "before" space in your soil properties chart.

8 Pour the water into the soil. Measure the amount of time it takes for the first drips to fall into the jar. Record the result in Table 1.

9 Once the water stops dripping, remove the bottle top. Use a new pH strip to measure the pH of the water in the jar. Record this measurement in the "after" space in Table 1 and note any differences in the appearance of the water before and after its filtering through the soil.

10 Discard the wet soil according to your teacher's instructions, and rinse the jar.

PARTICLE-TYPE TEST

11 Add water to the jar until it is two-thirds full. Pour in soil until the water level rises to the top of the jar, then replace the lid. Shake the jar, and set it to rest undisturbed on a countertop overnight.

12 The next day, observe the different soil layers. The sample should have separated into sand (on the bottom), silt (in the middle), and clay (on the top). Measure the height of each layer, as well as the overall height of the three layers. Record your measurements in Table 1.

13 Use the following formula to calculate the percentage of each kind of particle in the sample:

$$\frac{\text{height of layer}}{\text{total height of all layers}} \times 100$$

Record your results and all calculations in Table 1.

Observe and Analyze

1. **Record** Complete Table 1.

2. **Identify** How did steps 1–3 test your soil sample's pore space?

_____

_____

3. **Identify** How did steps 5–9 test your soil sample's drainage rate?

_____

_____

Conclude

1. **Evaluate** In step 3, you measured the amount of space between the soil particles in your sample. In step 8, you measured how quickly water passed through your sample. Are these two properties related? Explain your answer.

_____

_____

_____

2. **Evaluate** Would packing down or loosening up your soil sample change any of the properties you tested? Explain your answer.

_____

_____

_____

3. **Interpret** What happened to the pH of the water that passed through the soil? Why do you think that happened?

_____

_____

_____

4. **Analyze** Look at the percentages of sand, silt, and clay in your sample. How do the percentages help to explain the properties you observed and measured?

_____

_____

_____

_____

CHAPTER | ADDITIONAL INVESTIGATION
4 | **Soil Formation**

OVERVIEW AND PURPOSE

As you have read, soil is a mixture of weathered rock, air, water, and organic matter. Soil forms when rocks are changed by physical, chemical, and organic processes. In this investigation you will use what you have learned about soil to

- model some of the processes that form soil
- use your "soil" to make a soil profile

Procedure

1. Put on your safety goggles. Keep them on until you have completed this entire investigation.

2. Put 4 or 5 limestone chips into the small baby food jar. Add enough vinegar to cover the chips. Screw the lid on tightly and shake the jar for 2 minutes. Let the jar stand for at least 5 minutes.

3. Put the filter paper over the beaker. Pour the contents of the jar onto the filter paper. When the liquid has been completely filtered, remove the filter paper. Put it on a sunny windowsill to dry.

4. Break off some pieces from the sandstone. Put these pieces and any sand grains onto a sheet of newspaper.

5. Put 4 or 5 limestone chips and the rest of the sandstone into the pillowcase. CAUTION: Make sure everyone is well out of your way. Use the hammer to gently crush the rocks.

6. Empty the pillowcase onto another sheet of newspaper.

MATERIALS
- 10–15 limestone chips
- small baby food jar with lid
- 250 mL white vinegar
- filter paper
- 10-mL beaker
- crumbly sandstone
- fine-grained sand
- newspaper
- old pillowcase
- hammer
- plastic tube
- laboratory spatula
- clay-rich soil
- topsoil
- small sticks and twigs
- graduated cylinder
- water
- cork to seal plastic tube
- colored pencils
- metric ruler

TIME
45 minutes

7 Most soils have at least three distinct layers. A soil profile is a cutaway view of these different layers. One kind of soil profile is shown below. You will use this drawing and the materials from this investigation to make a soil profile.

A Horizon
   Mixture of organic matter, air, water, and coarse sediment

B Horizon
   Mixture of fine sediment such as clay, iron, calcium carbonate and oxides

C Horizon
   Weathered bedrock

Bedrock
   Shale, limestone, sandstone, and other rocks

Typical Soil Profile

8 Get the plastic tube. Put a few *unaltered* limestone chips into the bottom of the tube.

9 Add some large limestone pieces from the filter paper to the tube. Also put a few pieces of the crushed sandstone into the tube. Use the soil profile to determine how thick to make this layer.

10 Use the spatula to scrape off the powder from the filter paper. Put the powder into the tube. Put some of the sand grains in this layer as well. Add some clay. Again, use the soil profile to determine how thick to make this layer.

11 Add some topsoil and more sand grains to the tube. Break the twigs and sticks into small pieces so that they fit into the tube. Add them to your soil profile. Note that this layer is the thinnest layer in a soil profile.

12 Slowly add 5 mL of water to the tube.

13 Use the cork to seal the tube and stand it upright. Use your soil profile and the one above to answer the following questions.

Observe and Analyze

1. **Model** Which of the processes in this investigation are like the physical processes that form soil?

2. **Model** Which process in this investigation is similar to chemical processes that form soil?

3. **Analyze** Why does the first (bottom) layer in your profile contain unaltered rocks?

4. **Record** Use colored pencils and a metric ruler to draw your soil profile. Label and describe each layer.

CHAPTER 4
Weathering and Soil Formation

Conclude

1. **Explain** What kinds of organic matter are present in your soil?

   _____

   _____

2. **Identify Limits** How is your soil like actual soil? How is it different?

   _____

   _____

   _____

   _____

3. **Compare and Contrast** Do you think all soil profiles are the same? Why or why not?

   _____

   _____

   _____

   _____

SECTION
5.1 DATASHEET
Investigate Erosion

How does the effect of rainwater on sloping land differ from its effect on flat land?

MATERIALS Soil, 2 large trays, pitcher of water

PROCEDURE

1 Figure out how to use the soil, water, and trays to test the effects of rainwater on sloping land and on flat land.

2 Write up your procedure on a separate sheet of paper.

3 Carry out your experiment.

WHAT DO YOU THINK?

1. What were the results of your experiment? Did it work? Why or why not?

_____

_____

_____

2. What were the variables in your experiment?

_____

_____

3. What does your experiment demonstrate about erosion and running water?

_____

_____

CHALLENGE

How would you design an experiment to demonstrate the relationship between floods and erosion?

_____

_____

_____

_____

SECTION | DATASHEET
5.3 | Investigate Longshore Drift

How does sand move along a beach?

MATERIALS 2 or 3 books, coin

PROCEDURE

1. Prop up a book by placing another book underneath it.

2. Hold a coin with your finger against the bottom right corner of the book.

3. Gently flick the coin up the slope of the book at an angle. The coin should slide back down the book and fall off the bottom. If necessary, readjust the angle of the book and the strength with which you are flicking the coin.

4. Repeat step 3 several times. Observe the path the coin takes. Record your observations. Include a diagram that shows the general path the coin takes as it slides up and down the book.

_____

_____

WHAT DO YOU THINK?

1. What path did the coin take on its way up? On its way down?

_____

2. In this model of longshore drift, what represents the beach, what represents the sand, and what represents a wave?

_____

CHALLENGE

In this model, in which direction will the longshore current move? How could you change the model to change the direction of the current?

_____

_____

SECTION **5.4** | DATASHEET
Investigate Kettle Lake Formation

How do kettle lakes form?

MATERIALS shallow tray, ice cubes, modeling clay, sand, gravel, water

PROCEDURE

1 Use the tray, the ice cubes, and the other materials to model how sediment builds up around ice blocks.

2 Write a description of the process you used to make your model.

_____

_____

_____

_____

WHAT DO YOU THINK?

1. Describe how your model worked. What did you do first? What happened next?

_____

_____

_____

2. Did your model accurately represent the formation of kettle lakes? Did it work? Why or why not?

_____

_____

_____

3. What were the limitations of your model? Are there any aspects of kettle lake formation that are not represented? If so, what are they?

_____

_____

_____

_____

CHAPTER **5** | CHAPTER INVESTIGATION
Creating Stream Features

OVERVIEW AND PURPOSE

A view from the sky reveals that a large river twists and
bends in its channel. But as quiet as it might appear, the river
constantly digs and dumps Earth materials along its way.
This erosion and deposition causes twists and curves called
meanders, and a delta at the river's mouth. In this investigation
you will

- create a "river" in a stream table to observe the creation
  of meanders and deltas
- identify the processes of erosion and deposition

Problem

How does moving water create meanders and deltas?

MATERIALS
- stream table, with
  hose attachment or
  recirculating pump
- sieve (optional)
- wood blocks
- sand
- ruler
- water
- sink with drain
- pitcher (optional)
- bucket (optional)

Procedure

1 Arrange the stream table on a counter so that it drains into a sink or bucket. If
possible, place a sieve beneath the outlet hose to keep sand out of the drain. You
can attach the inlet hose to a faucet if you have a proper adapter. Or you can
gently pour water in with a pitcher or use a recirculating pump and a bucket.

2 Place wood blocks beneath the inlet end of the stream table so that the table tilts
toward the outlet at about a 20-degree angle. Fill the upper two-thirds of the
stream table nearly to the top with sand. Pack the sand a bit, and level the surface
with the edge of a ruler. The empty bottom third of the stream table represents the
lake or bay into which the river flows.

3 Using the end of the ruler, dig a gently curving trench halfway through the
thickness of the sand from its upper to its lower end.

4 Direct a gentle flow of tap water into the upper end of the trench. Increase the flow slightly when the water begins to move through the trench. You may have to try this several times before you find the proper rate of flow to soak the sand and fill the stream channel. Avoid adding so much water that it pools at the top before moving into the channel. You can also change the stream table's tilt.

5 Once you are successful in creating a river, observe its shape and any movement of the sand. Continue until the top part of the sand is completely washed away and your river falls apart. Scrape the sand back into place with the ruler, and repeat the procedure until you thoroughly understand the stream and sand movements.

Observe and Analyze

1. **Record** Diagram your stream-table setup, and make a series of drawings showing changes in your river over time. Be sure to label the river's features, as well as areas of erosion and deposition. Be sure to diagram the behavior of the sand at the river's mouth.

2. Record Write a record of the development of your river from start to finish. Include details such as the degree of tilt you used, your method of introducing water into the stream table, and features you observed forming.

_____

_____

_____

_____

_____

_____

Conclude

1. Evaluate How do you explain the buildup of sand at the mouth of your river? Use the words *speed, erosion,* and *deposition* in your answer. Did the slope of the stream change over time?

_____

_____

_____

_____

2. Interpret Where in your stream table did you observe erosion occurring? Deposition? What features did each process form?

_____

_____

_____

_____

3. Infer What might have occurred if you had increased the amount or speed of the water flowing into your river?

_____

_____

_____

4. **Identify Limits** In what ways was your setup a simplified version of what would actually occur on Earth? Describe the ways in which an actual stream would be more complex.

_____

_____

_____

_____

5. **Apply** Drawing on what you observed in this investigation, make two statements that relate the age of a stream to (1) the extent of its meanders and (2) to the size of its delta or alluvial fan.

_____

_____

_____

| ADDITIONAL INVESTIGATION
Rivers Change the Land

OVERVIEW AND PURPOSE

The moving water in a river changes Earth's landscape in different ways. A river can pick up sediments and carry them along its channel. When a river slows down, it may drop some of the sediments. In this lab, you will use what you have learned about moving water to

- observe how a river erodes and deposits sediments
- observe how the speed of a river affects the movement of sediments

Problem

How does a river change its channel?

Hypothesize

Form a hypothesis to explain how you think the speed of a river might affect the movement of sediments. Write your hypothesis as an "If . . . , then . . . , because . . . " statement.

_____

_____

_____

MATERIALS
- long, shallow cardboard box (at least 1 m × 50 cm × 5 cm)
- large, extra-strength trash bag just larger than the cardboard box
- duct tape
- metric ruler
- marking pen
- scissors
- rubber tubing (about 1 m long)
- brick or wooden block
- bucket
- fine-grained sand (about 5 kg)
- 5–10 pieces of pea-sized gravel
- 800-mL beaker
- water

TIME: 45 minutes

Procedure

1. Line the box with the trash bag. Push the bag completely against the bottom and sides of the box. Smooth out any wrinkles in the bag.

2. Use pieces of duct tape to hold the bag in place.

3. Use the ruler to mark a spot in the center of one of the short sides of the box. The spot should be about 1.5 cm from the bottom of the box.

4. From the inside of the box, use the scissors to carefully punch a hole at the mark. The hole should be just large enough for the rubber tubing.

5. Thread the tubing into the hole. Pull on the tubing until only about 2.5 cm of it is in the box.

6 Use the brick or block to prop up the model.

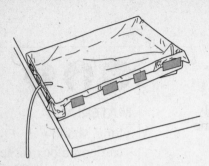

7 Put the bucket at the end of the tubing to catch the water that will flow down the model river.

8 Put the sand into the top 2/3 of the box. Level the sand, keeping it away from the tubing.

9 Use your first two fingers to carve a small channel into the sand.

10 Add a few pieces of gravel at different points in the channel.

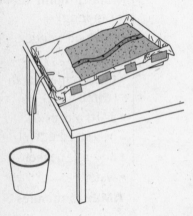

11 Fill the beaker with water. Hold it about 2.5 cm above your setup. Slowly pour the water into the channel at the top of the box.

12 Observe what happens to the sand and the gravel. Record your observations in the data table.

13 Allow the water to drain from the channel.

O F Repeat steps 11–13 three more times. Slightly increase the rate at which you pour the water into the channel each time.

DATA TABLE: RIVER FLOW OBSERVATIONS	
Trial	Observations
1	
2	
3	
4	

Observe and Analyze

1. Identify Variables What was your independent variable in this investigation?

_____

_____

_____

2. Identify Variables What was your dependent variable in this investigation?

_____

_____

_____

3. Observe During which trial was erosion the greatest?

_____

_____

_____

4. Observe What happened to the sand transported by the model river when the moving water reached the bottom of the channel?

_____

_____

_____

5. **Analyze** Was any of the gravel transported to the bottom of the channel? Why or why not?

_____

_____

_____

Conclude

1. **Compare** How did your hypothesis compare with your results?

_____

_____

_____

2. **Interpret** Use your results to describe three ways in which moving water can change a river channel.

_____

_____

_____

3. **Apply** Where along a real river channel do you think most erosion takes place?

_____

_____

_____

4. **Conclude** How does the speed of a river affect the movement of sediments?

_____

_____

_____

5. **Apply** How could you change your model to increase the amount of sediment carried by the river?

_____

_____

_____

6.1 | Investigate Earth's Different Layers

How can you model Earth's layers?

Materials clear plastic cup, small colored wooden beads, gravel, stirring stick, tap water

PROCEDURE

1 Put a layer of wooden beads about 1 centimeter thick at the bottom of a clear plastic cup.

2 Put a layer of gravel about 2 centimeters thick on top of the wooden beads. Stir the beads and gravel until they are well mixed.

3 Put another layer of gravel about 1 centimeter thick on top of the mix. Do NOT mix this layer of gravel.

4 SLOWLY fill the cup about two-thirds full of water. Be sure not to disturb the layers in the cup.

5 Stir the beads and gravel with the stick. Observe what happens.

WHAT DO YOU THINK?

1. What happened to the materials when you stirred them?

_____

2. How do you think this model represents the layers of Earth?

_____

_____

CHALLENGE

What could you add to the model to represent Earth's solid core?

_____

_____

CHAPTER 6
Plate Tectonics

6.3 | Investigate Magnetic Reversals

How can you map magnetic reversals?

MATERIALS string, bar magnet, masking tape, marking pen, sea-floor model

PROCEDURE

❶ Wrap one end of the string around the middle of the bar magnet. Tape the string in place.

❷ Place a small piece of tape on one end of the magnet. Label the tape *N* to represent north.

❸ Hold the bar magnet over one end of the sea-floor model. Move the magnet SLOWLY toward the other end of the sea-floor model. Record your observations.

WHAT DO YOU THINK?

1. What did the magnet reveal about the sea-floor model? Draw a diagram showing any pattern that you might have observed.

_____

2. Which part of the model represents the youngest sea floor? Which part represents the oldest sea floor?

_____

_____

CHALLENGE

If Earth's magnetic field had never reversed in the past, how would the sea-floor model be different?

_____

SECTION
DATASHEET
6.4 | Investigate Convergent Boundaries

How can you model converging plates?

MATERIALS clay in three or more colors, poster board, marker pens

PROCEDURE

1 Design your models using the materials listed. You can use the diagrams in your textbook as a guide.

2 Add more clay to your models if you need it.

WHAT DO YOU THINK?

1. Describe how your models worked. You can draw a picture of each model to go along with your description.

_____

_____

_____

2. How well did your models represent each type of zone? Did each model work? Why or why not?

_____

_____

_____

3. How would you modify your designs now that you have seen the results?

_____

_____

_____

CHAPTER
6 | CHAPTER INVESTIGATION
Convection Currents and Plate Movement

OVERVIEW AND PURPOSE

South America and Africa are drifting slowly apart. What powerful force could be moving these two plates? In this investigation you will

- observe the movement of convection currents
- determine how convection currents in Earth's mantle could move tectonic plates

Problem

How do convection currents in a fluid affect floating objects on the surface?

Hypothesize

Write a hypothesis to explain how convection currents affect floating objects. Your hypothesis should take the form of an "If . . . , then . . . , because . . ." statement.

MATERIALS
- oven-glass lasagna pan
- 2 bread pans or 2 bricks
- water
- 2 small candles
- matches
- liquid food coloring
- 2 sponges
- scissors
- 3–4 pushpins

CHAPTER 6
Plate Tectonics

Procedure

1 Use two overturned bread pans or two bricks to raise and support the glass lasagna pan. Fill the pan with water to a depth of 4 cm.

❷ Hold the food coloring bottle over the middle of the pan. Squeeze several drops of food coloring into the water. Be careful not to touch or disturb the water with the bottle or your hands. Write down your observations.

_____

_____

❸ Light the two candles and place them beneath the center of the pan. Then squeeze several more drops of food coloring into the middle of the pan.

❹ Observe what happens for a few minutes, and then write down your observations. After you have finished, blow out the candles and wait until the water cools.

_____

_____

❺ Moisten the two sponges. Cut one into the shape of South America and the other into the shape of Africa. Insert the pushpins.

❻ Place the sponges on top of the water in the center of the pan. Fit the two sponges together along their coastlines.

❼ Gently hold the sponges together until the water is still, then let go. Observe them for a few minutes and record what you saw.

_____

_____

❽ Light the candles again. Place them under the pan and directly beneath the two sponges.

9 Gently hold the sponges together again until the water heats up. Then carefully let go of the sponges, trying not to disturb the water.

10 Observe the sponges for a few minutes, and then record your observations.

_____

_____

Observe and Analyze

1. **Record** Draw diagrams to show how the food coloring and the sponges moved in cold water and in heated water. Use arrows to indicate any motion.

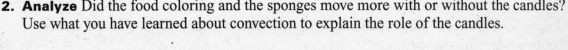

2. **Analyze** Did the food coloring and the sponges move more with or without the candles? Use what you have learned about convection to explain the role of the candles.

_____

_____

_____

Conclude

1. **Evaluate** Water is a fluid, but the asthenosphere is not. What properties of the asthenosphere allow it to move like a fluid and form convection currents?

_____

_____

2. **Compare and Contrast** In what ways is your setup like Earth's asthenosphere and lithosphere? In what ways is your setup different?

_____

_____

_____

_____

CHAPTER 6
Plate Tectonics

3. **Analyze** Compare your results with your hypothesis. Do your observations support your hypothesis? Why or why not?

_____

_____

_____

4. **Interpret** Write an answer to your problem statement.

_____

_____

_____

5. **Identify Controls** Did your experiment include controls? If so, what purpose did they serve here?

_____

_____

_____

6. **Apply** In your own words, explain how the African continent and the South American continent are drifting apart.

_____

_____

_____

_____

7. **Apply** Suppose you own an aquarium. You want to make sure your fish are warm whether they swim near the top or near the bottom of the aquarium. The pet store sells two types of heaters. One heater extends 5 cm below the water's surface. The other heater rests on the bottom of the aquarium. Based on what you learned in this activity, which heater would you choose, and why?

_____

_____

_____

CHAPTER | ADDITIONAL INVESTIGATION
6 | Magnetic Patterns on the Ocean Floor

OVERVIEW AND PURPOSE

When igneous rocks form, their iron minerals become magnetized in the direction of Earth's magnetic field. Earth's magnetic field changes with time. Today, Earth's magnetic field has normal polarity. At times in the past, the field has had reversed polarity. In this investigation you will use what you have learned about sea-floor spreading to

- model how changes in Earth's magnetic field are shown in rocks on the ocean floor
- demonstrate that magnetic data about Earth support the idea that the sea floor spreads apart

Problem

How can magnetism be used to support the idea that the sea floor spreads apart?

Hypothesize

Write a hypothesis to explain how changes in Earth's magnetic field can be used to show that spreading occurs along mid-ocean ridges. Write your hypothesis as an "If . . . , then .. because. . ." statement.

_____

_____

_____

MATERIALS
- pencil
- scissors
- metric ruler
- masking tape
- shoe box with lid
- colored pencils
- 2 bar magnets
- 2 large paper clips
- 2 magnetic compasses
- roll of plain wrapping paper or mailing paper

TIME: 45 minutes

**CHAPTER 6
Plate Tectonics**

Procedure

❶ Remove the paper from its cardboard tube. Re-roll it. Gently fold the roll of paper in the center and cut the roll in half. Trim the end of the rolls so that they will fit lengthwise into the shoe box, side by side. They should both be about 5 cm shorter than the long side of the box.

❷ Use the scissors to carefully cut a narrow slit down the center of the lid of the box. The slit should be about 1/2 centimeter wide.

3 Arrange the two rolls of paper in the bottom of the box.

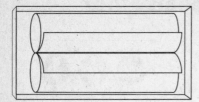

4 Work with another student to pull the ends of the paper through the slit. Secure the lid in place with masking tape.

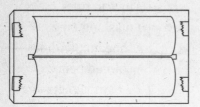

5 Place one bar magnet and one compass on either side of the slit in the box, as shown in the drawing. The slit is the "mid-ocean ridge" in your model.

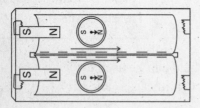

6 Use the metric ruler and a pencil to draw a straight line, about 15 cm long, on either side of the ridge. Make sure the lines are very close to the ridge.

7 Draw an arrow on each line to show the direction in which the compass needle is pointing. See the illustration above.

8 Remove the compasses and magnets from the top of the box.

9 Model sea-floor spreading by gently pulling 17 cm of paper from each roll through the slit. On a scale of 10 cm = 1 million years, this value represents the length of the Gilbert Epoch. Use this scale to determine your other "rates of spreading."

10 Repeat steps 5 through 8, but turn the magnets 180°.

11 Repeat this process—rotating the magnets, drawing the arrows, and modeling spreading—two more times. Remember to use the appropriate "rate of spreading" from the data in Table 1. Hint: Multiply each epoch length by 10 to figure out how many cm of paper to pull from the box.

TABLE 1. EARTH'S MAGNETIC EPOCHS			
Epoch	Polarity	Length of Epoch (millions of years)	Amount of Paper For Model (cm)
Gilbert	reversed	1.7	17
Gauss	normal	0.8	
Matuyama	reversed	1.8	
Brunhes	normal	0.7	

12 Remove the paper rolls from the box. Use the paper clips to attach the rolls to each other as shown below. This model represents the magnetic patterns that you would see on rocks on either side of a mid-ocean ridge.

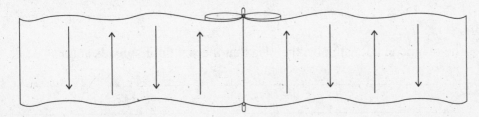

Observe and Analyze

1. **Model** Use the information in Table 1 to label your model. Use different colored pencils to color each of the four magnetic epochs. Include a color-coded key that explains which epoch is which on your model.

2. **Model** Why did you pull out the same length of paper on both sides when you made each set of magnetic lines?

_____

_____

3. **Model** What do the magnets represent?

_____

4. **Explain** Why did you rotate the magnets for each epoch?

_____

_____

5. **Observe** Which magnetic epoch was the longest? The shortest?

_____

_____

CHAPTER 6 Plate Tectonics

6. **Calculate** When did the Gilbert Epoch begin? Hint: The Brunhes Epoch is the most recent magnetic epoch.

_____

Conclude

1. **Explain** Where are the youngest igneous rocks on the ocean floor? The oldest?

_____
_____

2. **Infer** What kind of polarity will Earth's next magnetic epoch have?

_____
_____

3. **Apply** How does the magnetic data support the idea that the sea floor spreads apart?

_____
_____
_____

SECTION DATASHEET
7.1 | Investigate Faults

How can rocks move along faults?

MATERIALS 2 triangular blocks of wood, masking tape

PROCEDURE

1. Place one triangular block of wood against the other to form a rectangle.

2. Put two pieces of masking tape across both blocks. Draw a different pattern on each piece of tape. Break the tape where it crosses the blocks.

3. Keep the blocks in contact and slide one block along the other.

4. Repeat step 3 until you find three different ways the blocks can move relative to the other. Draw diagrams showing how the blocks moved. Include the tape patterns.

WHAT DO YOU THINK?

1. How can you use the tape patterns to find the relative directions in which the blocks were moved?

2. In each case, what sort of stress (such as pulling) did you put on the blocks?

CHALLENGE

Compare the ways you moved the blocks with the ways tectonic plates move at their boundaries.

CHAPTER 7
Earthquakes

SECTION
7.2 | DATASHEET
Earthquake Map

Tape a piece of string of the appropriate length to the back of the map at each earthquake location. What patterns do you observe.

Earthquake Location	Earthquake Depth	String Length (cm)
O	0–70	4
△	70–150	8
□	150–300	15

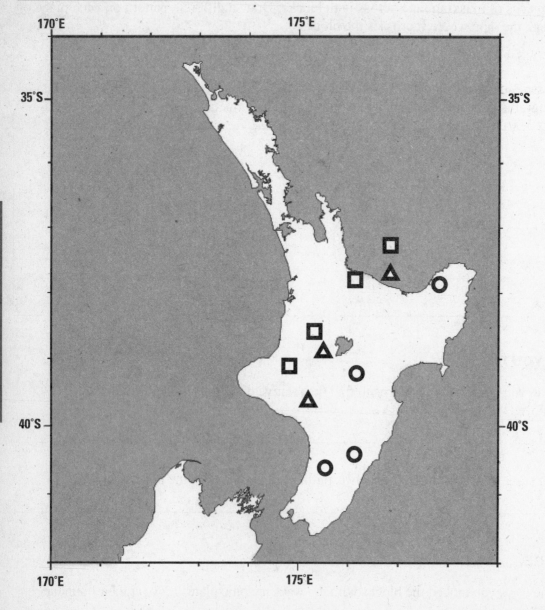

SECTION 7.2 | DATASHEET
Investigate Subduction-Zone Earthquakes

Why are some earthquakes deeper than others?

MATERIALS Earthquake Map, different colors of string, scissors, ruler, tape

PROCEDURE

1 Cut the first string into 4 pieces that are 4 cm long. Cut the second string into 3 pieces that are 8 cm long, and the third string into 4 pieces that are 15 cm long.

2 Use the key on the Earthquake Map to match string lengths with earthquake depths.

3 Tape one end of the pieces of string to the map at the earthquake locations. Always cover the same amount of string with tape.

4 Hold the map horizontally, with the strings hanging down. Observe the patterns of earthquake locations and depths.

WHAT DO YOU THINK?

1. What patterns among the strings do you observe? How do you explain them?

_____

_____

_____

2. How might the earthquake depths relate to the sinking of a tectonic plate in a subduction zone?

_____

_____

CHALLENGE

Draw a line on the map showing where the subduction zone might be at Earth's surface. How might the depths of the earthquakes be different if the subduction zone was on the other side of the island?

_____

_____

_____

CHAPTER 7
Earthquakes

CHAPTER | CHAPTER INVESTIGATION
7 | How Structures React in Earthquakes

OVERVIEW AND PURPOSE

In 1989 a magnitude 6.9 earthquake struck the San Francisco Bay area, killing 62 people and leaving 12,000 homeless. In 1988 a magnitude 6.9 earthquake occurred near Spitak, Armenia. There, nearly 25,000 people died and 514,000 lost their homes. The difference in the effects of these two earthquakes was largely due to differences in construction methods. In this investigation you will

- build a structure and measure how long it can withstand shaking on a shake table provided by your teacher
- explore methods of building earthquake-resistant structures

MATERIALS
- modeling clay
- stirrer straws
- piece of thin cardboard 15 cm on each side
- scissors
- ruler
- shake table

Problem

How can structures be built to withstand most earthquakes?

Hypothesize

Write a hypothesis to explain how structures can be built to withstand shaking. Your hypothesis should take the form of an "If . . . , then . . . , because . . ." statement.

_____

_____

Procedure

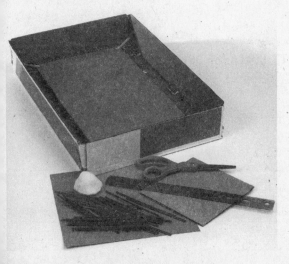

❶ Use stirrers joined with clay to build a structure at least 20 cm tall on top of the cardboard. Cut the stirrers if necessary.

CHAPTER 7
Earthquakes

2 Make a diagram of your structure.

3 Use Table 1 below.

TABLE 1. NUMBER OF TRIALS UNTIL COLLAPSE OF STRUCTURE		
Trial	Distance Platform Pulled to Side (cm)	Notes
1	2	
2	2	
3	2	
4	2	

CHAPTER 7
Earthquakes

④ Lift your structure by its cardboard base and place it on the shake-table platform. Pull the platform 2 centimeters to one side and release it.

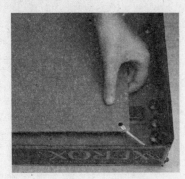

⑤ Repeat step 4 until the structure begins to collapse.

Observe and Analyze

1. **Record** Complete your data table and make notes about the collapse, including areas of possible weakness in your structure.

2. **Infer** Use your observations to design a structure that will better withstand shaking. Draw a diagram in the box below.

Conclude

1. **Interpret** Compare your results with your hypothesis. Do your observations support your hypothesis?

_____

_____

2. **Infer** How would you use the shake table to model earthquakes of different magnitudes? Draw a diagram in the box below.

_____

_____

3. **Identify Variables** How might your results differ if you always pulled the platform to the same side or if you pulled it to different sides?

_____

_____

_____

4. **Identify Limits** In what ways might a building's behavior during an earthquake differ from the behavior of your structure on the shake table?

_____

_____

_____

_____

5. **Compare** Examine the diagrams of the three structures that lasted longest in your class. What characteristics, if any, did they have in common?

_____

_____

_____

6. **Apply** Based on your results, write a list of recommendations for building earthquake-resistant structures.

_____

_____

_____

CHAPTER 7 | ADDITIONAL INVESTIGATION

Earthquake Depths

OVERVIEW AND PURPOSE

Earthquakes are common at plate boundaries. In this investigation, you will use what you have learned about plates and earthquakes to:

- make a model of earthquake depths
- describe how earthquake depths change along a convergent plate boundary

Problem

Do earthquake depths change as distance from a convergent plate boundary increases?

Hypothesize

Write a hypothesis to explain how you think earthquake depths might change along a plate descending into the mantle.

_____

_____

_____

MATERIALS
- tracing paper
- glue
- pencil
- scissors
- cardboard (40 cm × 20 cm)
- metric ruler
- small, thin nail
- yellow, green, red, and blue thread
- 12 small craft beads with holes (3 each of yellow, green, red, and blue)
- map that shows tectonic plate boundaries

TIME
45 minutes

Procedure

1 Trace the map of Alaska following in this book.

2 Glue the map onto the cardboard. Make sure the map is smooth.

3 While you wait for the glue to dry, study the earthquake data in Table 1. Classify the earthquakes into four groups. Use their depths to form the groups.

4 Decide which color of thread and bead you will use for each group. In Table 1, write your color choices for each earthquake.

5 On the map, plot the location of each earthquake. Put the number of the earthquake next to its location.

6 To model the depths, use a scale of 1 cm = 5 km. Compute the scale depths by dividing each actual depth by 5. Write your answers in Table 1.

7 Carefully use the nail to punch a hole at the location of the first earthquake.

8 Tie a bead of the color you have chosen to represent the first earthquake in the table to the thread of the same color.

CHAPTER 7
Earthquakes

⑨ Measure and cut the thread so that it is slightly longer than the final length you need.

⑩ Push the thread through the hole in the map from underneath the map until the bead hangs at the appropriate length under the map.

⑪ Fasten the thread in place by taping its top end to the surface of the map.

⑫ Repeat steps 8–11 for the other earthquakes.

TABLE 1. SOME ALASKAN EARTHQUAKES					
Earthquake	Color of Thread and Beads	Latitude	Longitude	Depth of Earthquakes (km)	Scale Depth (cm)
1		50.4 N	174.6W	11	
2		51.2 N	176.2 W	20	
3		50.7 N	178.4 W	33	
4		53.1 N	168.5 W	74	
5		53.6 N	167.1 W	105	
6		52.0 N	179.8 W	123	
7		55.7 N	163.0 W	150	
8		55.4 N	162.1 W	156	
9		56.1 N	162.3 W	171	
10		59.9 N	153.7 W	172	
11		58.9 N	171.6 W	218	
12		56.6 N	160.2 W	228	

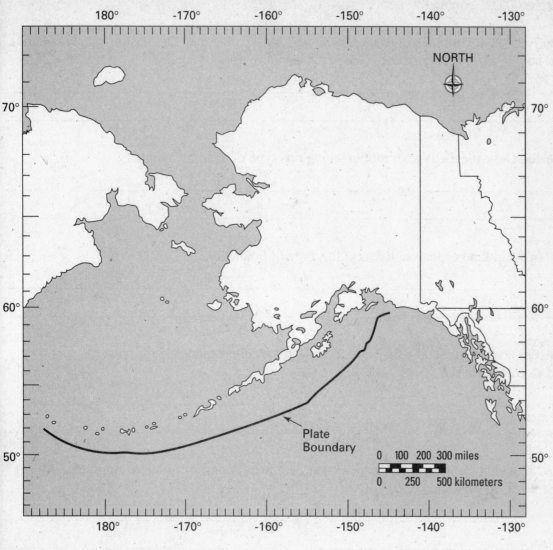

Observe and Analyze

1. Analyze Where did the deepest earthquakes take place?

_____

_____

2. Analyze Where did the shallowest earthquakes occur?

_____

_____

3. Recognize Patterns Describe how the earthquake depths changed along this plate boundary.

_____

_____

_____

Conclude

1. **Classify** Look at your map of Alaska. Now find Alaska on a map that shows plate boundaries. What kind of plate boundary exists along the southern edge of Alaska?

   _____

   _____

2. **Describe** Describe the type of motion along this type of tectonic boundary.

   _____

   _____

3. **Explain** What kind of feature forms at this type of boundary?

   _____

   _____

4. **Identify** The movement of which two tectonic plates are responsible for most of Alaska's earthquakes?

   _____

   _____

5. **Infer** An earthquake's epicenter is located at 54.4 N latitude and 170.0 W longitude. Infer the depth of the earthquake.

   _____

   _____

SECTION | DATASHEET
8.1 | Investigate Fault-Block Mountains

How do fault-block mountains form?

MATERIALS 3 triangular blocks, 3 rectangular blocks

PROCEDURE

1 Use the triangular blocks to demonstrate how movements along normal faults form two mountains separated by a valley. Start with the blocks arranged as shown in your textbook. Move the outer blocks apart to form two mountains separated by a valley. Draw a diagram of your results.

2 Use the rectangular blocks to demonstrate how a row of tilted fault-block mountains forms along normal faults. (Hint: You can tilt the blocks as they move.) Draw a diagram of your results.

WHAT DO YOU THINK?

1. How do your diagrams show that fault-block mountains form as the crust is being stretched?

   _____

   _____

2. Along which type of plate boundary would fault-block mountains be most likely to form—divergent, convergent, or transform? Explain.

   _____

   _____

CHALLENGE

Why do fault-block mountains not form at strike-slip faults?

_____

_____

CHAPTER 8
Mountains and Volcanoes

SECTION
8.3 | DATASHEET
Mt. Rainier Mudflows

How does the shape of the land affect mudflows?

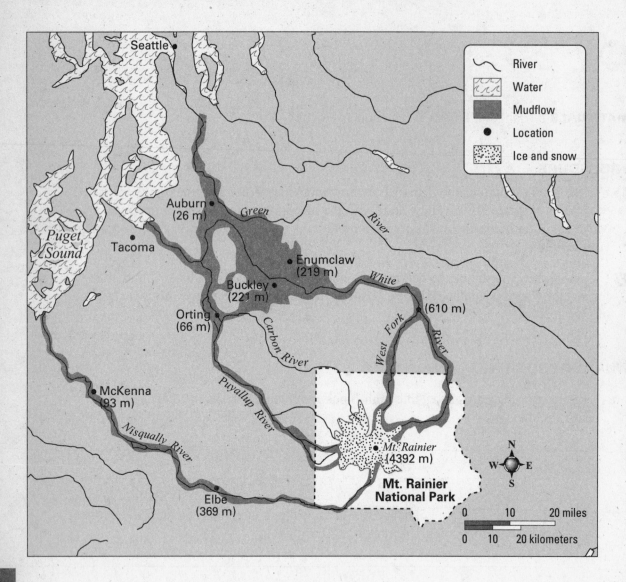

SECTION
8.3 | DATASHEET
| **Investigate Mudflows**

How does the shape of the land affect mudflows?

MATERIALS Map of Mount Rainier Mudflows

PROCEDURE

❶ Look at the map of Mount Rainier mudflows. Observe the relationship between the paths of rivers and the paths of the mudflows.

❷ Write the number of towns shown within the boundaries of mudflow areas.

_____

❸ Write the differences in elevation between the following locations: the top of Mount Rainier and the point where the West Fork joins the White River, the point where the rivers join and the town of Buckley, and the towns of Buckley and Auburn. Where is the land steepest?

_____

_____

❹ On another sheet of paper, explain why in some areas mudflows have followed rivers and in other areas mudflows have spread out.

WHAT DO YOU THINK?

1. What three factors are most important in causing mudflows to start near the top of Mount Rainier and flow long distances?

_____

_____

2. How likely are future mudflows to follow the same paths as earlier mudflows? Why?

_____

_____

CHALLENGE

The largest mudflow starting on Mount Rainier moved at about 22 kilometers per hour (14 mi/h) and covered the land to an average depth of 6 meters (20 ft). Describe the steps you would take to protect people from a similar mudflow in the same area.

_____

_____

CHAPTER 8
Mountains and Volcanoes

CHAPTER 8 | CHAPTER INVESTIGATION
Make Your Own Volcanoes

OVERVIEW AND PURPOSE

Scientists who have never been to a particular volcano can estimate how steep a climb it would be to its top. All they need to know is what type of volcano it is. Volcanoes vary not only in size but also in slope, or the steepness of their sides. The three main types of volcanoes—cinder cones, shield volcanoes, and composite volcanoes—are very different in size and shape. In this investigation you will

- make models of volcanoes and measure their slopes
- determine how the types of materials that form a volcano affect how steep it can get

MATERIALS
- 375 mL plaster of Paris
- 180 mL water
- 500 mL gravel
- 3 cardboard pieces
- two 250-mL paper cups
- stirrer
- ruler
- protractor

Problem

What does a volcano's slope reveal about the materials that formed it?

Hypothesize

Write a hypothesis to explain how a volcano's slope is related to the materials it is made of. Your hypothesis should take the form of an "If . . . , then . . . , because . . . " statement.

_____

_____

Procedure

❶ Mix 125 mL of plaster of paris with 60 mL of water in a paper cup. Stir the mixture well. Work quickly with the mixture, because it will harden quickly.

CHAPTER 8
Mountains and Volcanoes

2 Pour the mixture onto a piece of cardboard from a height of 2–3 cm.
Write "cone A" on the cardboard and set it aside.

3 Fill another paper cup with gravel. Slowly pour the gravel onto a second piece
of cardboard from a height of about 10 cm. Label this model "cone B" and set
it aside.

4 In a cup, mix the rest of the plaster of Paris with the rest of the water. Fill the
other paper cup with gravel. Pour a small amount of the plaster mixture onto the
third piece of cardboard, then pour some gravel on top. Repeat until all the plaster
mixture and gravel have been used. Label this model "cone C" and set it aside
until the plaster in both cone A and cone C has hardened (about 20 min).

5 Use Table 1 below.

TABLE 1. VOLCANO MODEL AND SLOPE		
Cone	Drawing of Cone	Slope (in degrees)
A		
B		
C		

Observe and Analyze

1. **Measure** Use the protractor to measure the approximate slope of each cone.

2. **Record** Complete Table 1.

3. **Observe** Compare the appearances of the cones. Record your observations.

4. **Compare** How different are the slopes of the cones?

Conclude

1. **Connect** Which volcanic materials do the plaster mixture and the gravel represent?

2. **Identify Variables** What is the relationship between the cones' slopes and the materials they are made of?

3. **Analyze** Compare your results with your hypothesis. Do your data support your hypothesis?

4. **Interpret** Which type of volcano does each model represent?

5. **Draw Conclusions** Which of your models represents a volcano that cannot grow as large as the others? Explain.

CHAPTER 8 Mountains and Volcanoes

6. **Predict** What factors might cause the slopes of real volcanoes to be different from those of your models?

_____

_____

7. **Apply** If you were a scientist, what information, in addition to slope, might you need in order to determine a volcano's type?

_____

_____

8. **Apply** How could the method you used to make a model of a cinder cone be used to show how the slope of a hill or mountain contributes to a landslide?

_____

_____

CHAPTER
ADDITIONAL INVESTIGATION

8 | Modeling Magma Movement

OVERVIEW AND PURPOSE

A magma chamber is a large, underground area that contains molten rock. Some of this molten rock, or magma, can reach Earth's surface during a volcanic eruption. Some of the magma stays beneath Earth's surface and hardens into rock underground. In this investigation, you will use what you've learned about volcanoes to

- make a model volcano
- model how magma can move within a volcano

Problem

How can magma movement be modeled?

Hypothesize

Write a hypothesis to explain how you think magma might move through a volcano.

_____

_____

_____

Procedure

1 Make the gelatin according to the directions on the package. Be careful when using the heat source. Note that it is important for the gelatin to completely dissolve before you pour the mixture into the bowl.

2 Spray the medium-sized bowl with a *very small* amount of the nonstick cooking spray.

3 Carefully pour the gelatin into the bowl. Put the bowl into a refrigerator until the gelatin is set.

4 Mix two or three spoonfuls of red food coloring in a cup of cold water. This is your model magma.

5 Use the paint cans to prop up the pizza pan or cookie sheet as shown in the illustration below.

6 Put the large plastic storage box under the set-up to collect any spills.

MATERIALS

- water
- cooking pot
- refrigerator
- red pencil
- plastic knife
- 2 1-gallon paint cans
- 2 measuring cups
- thin plastic syringe
- wooden spoon
- large spoon
- red food coloring
- large plastic storage box
- nonstick cooking spray
- heat-resistant lab gloves
- hot plate or other heat source
- medium-sized plastic bowl
- 4 large envelopes unflavored gelatin
- pizza pan or cookie sheet with holes in the bottom

TIME

45 minutes (once gelatin has set)

7 When the gelatin is completely set, carefully turn the bowl over onto the center of the pizza pan or cookie sheet. Be careful not to fracture the model volcano.

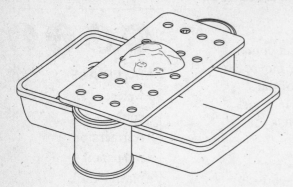

8 Fill the thin syringe with "magma." Note that you will be injecting the magma into the bottom of your volcano.

9 Insert half of the syringe into a hole at the center of the pizza pan or cookie sheet.

10 Slowly inject the "magma" into the volcano and observe what happens. Write down your observations in the data table. Plot the location of the injection on the diagram on the next page.

11 Carefully remove the syringe so that you don't fracture your model. If fractures do form, avoid them when making future injections.

12 Repeat steps 8–11 at least nine more times. Make some injections close to the first injection. Make one or two injections near the edges of your model volcano. Remember to plot the location of each injection on the circle on the next page.

DATA TABLE: MAGMA MOVEMENT IN A MODEL VOLCANO	
Trial	**Description of Magma Movement**
1	
2	
3	
4	
5	
6	
7	
8	
9	
10	

CHAPTER 8
Mountains and Volcanoes

View of Model Volcano Showing Where Each Injection Was Made

Observe and Analyze

1. **Infer** Why did you inject the magma from below?

_____
_____
_____
_____

2. **Analyze** In general, how did the model magma move through the model volcano?

_____
_____

3. **Explain** Did the magma injected near the edges of the volcano behave differently from magma injected into the center of the structure? Explain.

_____
_____
_____

4. **Model** Use the knife to cut your model volcano in half from top to bottom. Draw a side-view diagram of one half of your model volcano. Use a red pencil to draw the magma pipes.

CHAPTER 8
Mountains and Volcanoes

5. **Model** Use the knife to cut about 3 cm off the top of your model volcano. Draw a top view diagram of what you see. Again, use a red pencil to draw the magma.

Conclude

1. **Infer** What do you think might have happened if you had injected the magma too quickly into the model volcano?

_____

_____

_____

2. **Conclude** Observe your volcano again. Describe how the model magma moved in relation to where it was injected.

_____

_____

_____

_____

3. **Infer** In a real volcano, what might happen to some of the magma as it rises and cools?

_____

_____

_____

4. **Apply** Magma that hardens at angles in relation to existing rocks is called a dike. Magma that hardens parallel to existing rocks is called a sill. Which of these structures was modeled in this investigation? Explain your answer.

_____

_____

_____

_____

SECTION
9.1 | DATASHEET
Tree Cross-Section

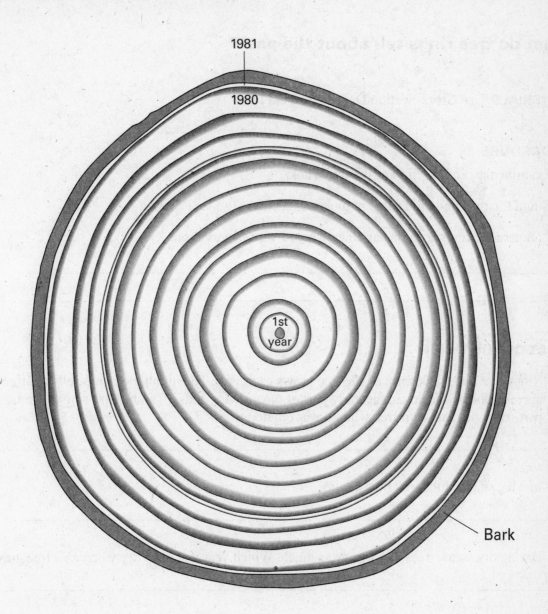

1981

1980

1st
year

Bark

SECTION | DATASHEET
9.1 | Investigate Learning from Tree Rings

What do tree rings tell about the past?

MATERIALS Tree Cross-Section Datasheet, hand lens

PROCEDURE

❶ Examine the cross-section of the tree trunk.

❷ Count the dark and light rings in the cross section.

❸ Compare the rings with one another. Record your observations.

_____

_____

WHAT DO YOU THINK?

1. Rings in a tree trunk form as the tree grows each year. The number of rings tells the tree's age. A light ring forms in the early part of the growing season, and a dark ring in the later part. How old was your tree when it was cut down?

   _____

2. In what year did the tree first grow?

   _____

3. During dry years, trees don't grow as much. Which year was very dry where this tree grew?

   _____

CHALLENGE

During what part of the growing season was this tree probably cut down? How do you know?

_____

_____

_____

SECTION **9.2** | DATASHEET
Investigate Relative and Absolute Age

How can newspapers model rock layers?

MATERIALS 5 or more newspapers with different dates, 2 pencils

PROCEDURE

❶ Have one person in your group arrange the newspapers in a pile with the oldest newspaper on the bottom and the newest on top.

❷ After the newspapers are stacked, place one pencil between two newspapers and the other pencil between two different newspapers. Use the model to answer the questions below.

WHAT DO YOU THINK?

1. If the newspapers were really placed on the stack on the days they were published, which pencil has probably been there longer?

   _____

2. Look at the dates on the newspapers. Now what can you say about when the pencils were placed on the stack?

   _____

   _____

CHALLENGE

How does what you could tell about the "ages" of the pencils before looking at the dates differ from what you could tell after looking?

_____

_____

_____

CHAPTER | DATASHEET
9 | **Geologic Time Scale**

Fill out the chart below. Some measurements are already filled in for you.
Scale: 1 millimeter = 1 million years

Division of Geologic Time	Millions of Years Ago It Began	Measurement
Eons		
Hadean	4600	4.6 meters
Archean	3800	
Proterozoic	2500	
Phanerozoic	544	
Eras		
Paleozoic	544	54.4 centimeters
Mesozoic	248	
Cenozoic	65	
Periods		
Cambrian	544	54.4 centimeters
Ordovician	490	
Silurian	443	
Devonian	417	
Carboniferous	354	
Permian	290	
Triassic	248	
Jurassic	206	
Cretaceous	144	
Tertiary	65	
Quaternary	2	
Epochs		
Paleocene	65	6.5 centimeters
Eocene	55	
Oligocene	34	
Miocene	24	
Pliocene	5	
Pleistoscene	2	
Holocene	0.01	

CHAPTER 9

CHAPTER INVESTIGATION

Geologic Time

OVERVIEW AND PURPOSE

Geologists use information from rocks, fossils, and other natural evidence to piece together the history of Earth. The geologic time scale organizes Earth's history into intervals of time called eons, eras, periods, and epochs. In this investigation you will

- construct a model of the geologic time scale
- place fossil organisms and geologic events in the correct sequence on the timeline

MATERIALS

- geologic time scale conversion chart
- adding-machine paper 5 meters long
- scissors
- colored markers, pens, or pencils
- metric tape measure or meter stick
- sticky notes

Procedure

1. Lay the adding-machine paper out in front of you. At the far right end of the strip write "TODAY" lengthwise along the edge.

2. Starting from the TODAY mark, measure back 4.6 meters, or 4600 million years. Label this point "AGE OF EARTH." Cut off excess paper.

3. Fold the paper in half lengthwise and then fold it in half lengthwise again. Unfold the paper. The creases should divide your paper into four rows.

4. At the far left end of the strip, label each of the four rows as shown.

CHAPTER 9
Views of Earth's Past

⑤ Using the geologic time scale in the your book, complete the geologic time scale conversion chart below. Use the conversion 1 mm = 1 million years to change the number of years for each eon, era, period, and epoch on the chart into metric measurements (millimeters, centimeters, and meters).

GEOLOGIC TIME SCALE CONVERSION CHART		
Division of Geologic Time	**Millions of Years Ago**	**Measurement**
Eons		
Hadean	4600	4.6 meters
Archean	3800	
Proterozoic	2500	
Phanerozoic	544	
Eras		
Paleozoic		
Mesozoic		
Cenozoic		
Periods		
Cambrian		
Ordovician		
Silurian		
Devonian		
Carboniferous		
Permian		
Triassic		
Jurassic		
Cretaceous		
Tertiary		
Quaternary		
Epochs		
Paleocene		
Eocene		
Oligocene		
Miocene		
Pliocene		
Pleistocene		
Holocene		

6   Using the numbers from your chart, measure each eon. Start each measurement from the TODAY line and measure back in time. For example, the Archean eon started 3800 million years ago, so measure back 3.8 meters from today. Mark that distance and write "ARCHEAN EON." Do the same for the other eons.

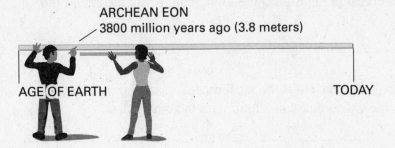

ARCHEAN EON
3800 million years ago (3.8 meters)

AGE OF EARTH   TODAY

7   Repeat step 5 to measure and label the eras, periods, and epochs.

8   After all the eons, eras, periods, and epochs are measured and labeled, use the same measuring technique to add the fossils and events from the table below.

TABLE 1. IMPORTANT EVENTS IN EARTH'S HISTORY	
Fossils and Events	**Time (millions of years ago)**
First trilobite	554
First mammal	210
Greatest mass extinction	248
First green algae	1000
Early humans	2
Extinction of dinosaurs	65
First life forms	3800
Flowering plants	130

9   Draw pictures of the fossils and events or write the names of the fossils and events on the timeline. If you do not have space to write directly on the timeline, write on sticky notes and then place the sticky notes at the correct positions on the timeline.

Observe and Analyze

1. **Compare and Contrast** The time from 4.6 billion years ago up until the beginning of the Phanerozoic eon is called Precambrian time. Find the part of your timeline that represents Precambrian time. How does Precambrian time compare in length with the rest of the geologic time scale?

_____

2. **Compare and Contrast** The Cenozoic era is the most recent era, and it includes the present. How does the Cenozoic era compare in length with the other eras?

_____

3. **Interpret** Where on the timeline are the two major extinction events?

_____

4. **Infer** What does the location of the two major extinction events suggest about how geologists divided the time scale into smaller units?

_____

_____

Conclude

1. **Interpret** Where are most of the life forms that you placed on your time line grouped?

_____

2. **Infer** Judging by the locations of most of the life forms on your timeline, why do you think the shortest era on the timeline—the Cenozoic era—has been divided into so many smaller divisions?

_____

_____

3. **Evaluate** What limitations or difficulties did you experience in constructing or interpreting this model of the geologic time scale?

_____

_____

4. **Apply** Think about the relationship between fossils, rock layers, and the geologic time scale. Why do you think the geologists who first constructed the geologic time scale found it difficult to divide the first three eons into smaller time divisions?

_____

_____

CHAPTER
9 | ADDITIONAL INVESTIGATION
Fossils

OVERVIEW AND PURPOSE

As you have read, fossils are the preserved traces or remains of once-living organisms. In this investigation you will use what you have learned about fossils to

- make model fossils
- distinguish between a mold and cast fossil
- describe the differences between mold and cast fossils

MATERIALS
- modeling clay
- plaster of Paris
- petroleum jelly or cooking oil
- small paper cups (6 oz)
- objects such as leaves, dead insects, shells, or twigs, to make imprints
- water
- container to mix plaster
- paper towels
- toothpicks
- markers
- hand lens

TIME
45 minutes

Procedure

1 Cut the top off of two paper cups, leaving approximately 3 cm to the bottom. Write your name on the bottoms of the cups.

2 Press clay into the bottom of the cup, leaving about 1 cm of space at the top of the clay. Use your fingers to smooth out the clay as much as possible.

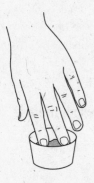

3 Select 2 objects to use to make your model fossils. Use one object for each cup.

4 Lightly coat the objects in petroleum jelly or cooking oil.

5 Carefully press the objects into the clay, and then remove the objects. If the image is unclear, you may smooth the clay and try again.

6 Make the plaster of Paris. You need only a small amount for your cups. Your teacher may make enough for the whole class.

7 Pour the plaster into the paper cups, on top of the clay with impressed images. Your teacher may come around and pour the plaster for the whole class.

8 Let plaster set for 2–3 minutes until it is stiff enough to hold the shape of an object.

9 Once the plaster is stiff, carefully press the object into the plaster and let sit for a minute or two.

10 Carefully remove the object.

11 Let all models sit undisturbed for at least 30 min.

12 When the plaster is dry, peel the paper cup from the plaster and clay. Carefully remove the clay from the plaster. Write your name on your model fossils.

Observe and Analyze

1. **Infer** Which of your model fossils represent cast fossils, and which represent molds? Draw a picture of each and label the model fossils *cast* or *mold*.

2. **Compare** Make two lists of observations, one for a model cast fossil and another for a model mold fossil. Use your list to compare and contrast molds and casts.

_____

_____

3. **Explain** Draw a sketch of the model you made. How does your model represent the way fossils form?

_____

_____

4. **Explain** How does the model you made differ from the way fossils actually form?

_____

_____

_____

Conclude

1. **Apply** Examine one of your model mold fossils. If it was a real fossil, how might it have formed?

_____

_____

2. **Apply** Examine one of your model cast fossils. If it was a real fossil, how might it have formed?

_____

_____

_____

3. **Infer** Suppose that another rock layer formed on top of the plaster. What kind of fossil might form?

_____

_____

4. **Apply** Exchange fossils with one of your classmates. Try to find someone who you did not see make the model fossil, so you do not know what objects the person used. Imagine that you are a scientist who found these fossils. Make sketches and record detailed observations of the fossils. What can you tell about the object that the fossil represents? Return the fossil to your classmate when you are done.

SECTION
10.1 DATASHEET
Investigate Fossil Fuels

Why does an oil spill do so much harm?

MATERIALS vegetable oil, large pan (at least 22 cm), plastic-foam ball (about 5 cm), eyedropper

PROCEDURE

1 Fill the pan about halfway with water. Using an eyedropper, carefully add 10 drops of oil in the middle of the pan. Rock the pan gently.

2 Observe what happens to the drops of oil over the next 2 min. Record your observations.

_____

_____

3 Place the plastic-foam ball in the oil slick, wait a few seconds, then carefully lift the ball out again. Examine it and record your observations.

_____

_____

WHAT DO YOU THINK?

1. What happened when the drop of oil came in contact with the water?

_____

_____

2. What might happen to an animal that swims through spilled oil?

_____

_____

CHALLENGE

Think of a way to clean up the oil slick on the water. Discuss your ideas with your teacher before you test your cleaning method. Record your ideas below.

_____

_____

CHAPTER 10
Natural Resources

SECTION
10.2 | DATASHEET
Investigate Conservation

How can you tell which bulb wastes less energy?

MATERIALS 2 table lamps, incandescent light bulb, fluorescent light bulb, 2 thermometers, pen or pencil

PROCEDURE

❶ Figure out how you are going to test which light bulb—incandescent or fluorescent—wastes less energy.

❷ Write up your procedure here.

_____

_____

_____

_____

_____

_____

❸ Conduct your experiment and record your results.

WHAT DO YOU THINK?

1. What were the variables in your experiment?

_____

_____

2. What were the results of your experiment?

_____

_____

_____

3. How does your experiment demonstrate which light bulb is more energy efficient?

_____

_____

_____

CHAPTER 10
Natural Resources

CHAPTER
10 | CHAPTER INVESTIGATION
Wind Power

OVERVIEW AND PURPOSE

Early windmills were designed mainly to pump water and grind flour. In this investigation you will use what you have learned about renewable resources to

- build a model windmill and use it to lift a small weight
- improve its performance by increasing the strength of the wind source

Problem

What effect will increasing the wind strength have on the lifting power of a model windmill?

Hypothesize

After completing step 7 in the procedure, write a hypothesis to explain what you think will happen in the next two sets of trials. Your hypothesis should take the form of an "if . . . , then . . . , because" statement.

MATERIALS
- half of a file folder
- metric ruler
- quarter
- scissors
- brass paper fastener
- drinking straw
- pushpin
- pint carton
- masking tape
- 30 cm of string
- small paper clip
- clock or stopwatch
- small desktop fan

CHAPTER 10
Natural Resources

Procedure

❶ Cut a 15-cm square from a manila file folder. With a ruler, draw lines from each corner of the square toward the center, forming an X. Where the lines cross, use a quarter to draw a circle. Cut inward along the lines from the four corners, stopping at the small circle. Punch a hole in each corner and in the center of the circle.

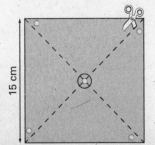

2 Bend the cardboard to align the holes. Push a brass paper fastener through the holes toward the back of the pinwheel. Do not flatten the metal strips of the fastener.

3 Use a pushpin to poke a hole through a straw, about 4 cm from the end. Then push the metal strips through the hole and flatten them at right angles to the straw. Fold the tip of the straw over, and tape it to the rest of the straw.

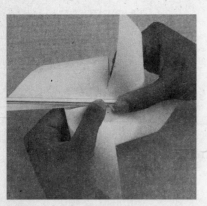

4 Cut the spout portion off the top of the pint carton. Punch two holes on opposite sides of the carton as shown. Make sure the holes line up and are large enough for the straw to turn easily.

5 Slide the straw through the holes. Tape the string to the end of the straw. Tie a small paper clip (weight) to the other end of the string.

6 Test the model by blowing on the blades. Describe what happens to the weight.

7 Run three trials of the lifting power of the model windmill as you blow on the blades. Have a classmate use a stopwatch or clock with a second hand to time the trials. Record the results in Table 1. Average your results.

8 Vary the strength of the wind by using a desktop fan at different speeds to turn the windmill's blades. Remember to record your hypothesis explaining what you think will happen in the next two sets of trials.

TABLE 1. TIME TO LIFT WEIGHT		
Wind Force Used	Trial Number	Time (sec)
Student powered	1	
	2	
	3	
	Average	
	1	
	2	
	3	
	Average	
	1	
	2	
	3	
	Average	

CHAPTER 10
Natural Resources

Observe and Analyze

1. **Model** Draw a picture of the completed windmill. What happens to the weight when the blades turn?

2. **Identify Variables** What method (variable) did you use to increase the wind strength? Add a sketch of this method to your picture to illustrate the experimental procedure.

_____

_____

3. **Record Observations** Make sure Table 1 is complete.

4. **Compare** How did the average times it took to raise the weight at different wind strengths differ?

_____

_____

_____

Conclude

1. **Interpret** Answer the question posed in the problem.

_____

_____

_____

2. **Analyze** Did your results support your hypothesis?

_____

_____

_____

3. **Identify Limits** What limitations or sources of error could have affected the experimental results?

_____

_____

_____

_____

4. **Apply** Wind farms are used to generate electricity in some parts of the country. What might limit the usefulness of wind power as an energy source?

_____

_____

_____

_____

CHAPTER
10 | ADDITIONAL INVESTIGATION
Solar Houses

OVERVIEW AND PURPOSE

A solar building captures energy from the Sun to provide heat and sometimes electricity for the building. In this investigation you will use what you have learned about solar energy to

- construct simple models of three solar houses
- observe how different colors affect the houses' ability to capture and retain (keep) heat

Problem

How does color affect the ability of a building to capture and retain heat?

Hypothesize

How do you think the color of a building will affect the rate at which the building can absorb heat? Write a hypothesis to explain the effect of color. Your hypothesis should be an "if, . . . then, . . . because" sentence.

_____

_____

MATERIALS
- 3 identical shoe boxes with lids
- ruler
- scissors
- plastic wrap
- masking tape
- 3 sheets of construction paper: 1 black, 1 white, 1 other
- transparent tape
- 3 thermometers
- clock or watch
- sunlight or artificial light source
- 3 different colored pencils

TIME: 45 minutes

CHAPTER 10
Natural Resources

Procedure

1 Use the ruler to mark off a rectangular window on one of the short sides of one box. Make sure the window will not be blocked when the lid is on the box.

2 Carefully use the scissors to cut out the window.

3 Use the scissors to punch a hole into the center of the other short side of the box. Make sure the hole is just large enough for one of the thermometers.

4 Repeat steps 1–3 for the other two boxes. Make sure the windows and holes are identical in size and that they are in the same position on each box. (You can use the window you cut out of the first box as a stencil. Trace the window onto the other two boxes so that they are the same size.)

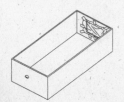

5 Cut three pieces of plastic wrap that are just slightly larger than the windows. Use the transparent tape to secure one piece of wrap to the inside of each window. Make sure all of the edges of the wrap are taped down.

6 Use the masking tape to secure a lid onto each box so that the box is completely sealed.

7 Use the transparent tape to cover one of the boxes with the black construction paper. Do not cover the window.

8 Use the scissors to remove the construction paper from the small hole.

9 Repeat steps 7 and 8. Cover one box with white construction paper and one box with the other color.

10 Carefully slide a thermometer halfway into the small hole in each box, as shown in the illustration.

11 Let the boxes sit until the thermometers are reading the same temperature. The boxes should not be in the light. Once the temperature is the same in all three boxes, record the temperature in Table 1.

TABLE 1. CHANGES IN TEMPERATURE			
Time (min)	Temperature (°): Black House	Temperature (°): White House	Temperature (°): _____ House
0			
5			
10			
15			
20			
25			

12 Put all three boxes onto a sunny windowsill or under an artificial light source. Make sure each box is facing the same way and that each box is receiving the same amount of light.

13 Measure and record the temperature in each house every 5 minutes for 25 minutes.

Observe and Analyze

1. **Identify Variables** What was the independent variable in this investigation? What was the dependent variable?

   _____

   _____

2. **Model** Why was it necessary to make the holes and windows the same size?

   _____

   _____

3. **Explain** Why did you completely seal the boxes before wrapping them in paper?

   _____

   _____

4. **Graph** Use the colored pencils to graph the results of this investigation below. Label your graph. Also include a title and a key that shows which set of data belongs to which house.

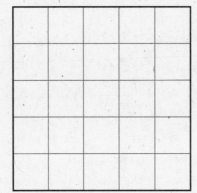

5. **Sequence** Use your graph to rank the houses according to their ability to absorb solar energy.

   _____

   _____

CHAPTER 10
Natural Resources

Conclude

1. **Explain** Why did you need to wait for the temperature to be the same in each house before you began to measure changes in temperature?

_____

_____

2. **Conclude** Which house would capture the most solar energy the quickest?

_____

3. **Conclude** Which of your model houses do you think would lose solar energy the slowest?

_____

4. **Apply** How could you change your own family home to make it more energy-efficient? Think about the results of this investigation.

_____

_____

CHAPTER 10
Natural Resources

SECTION | DATASHEET
11.1 | Investigate the Water Cycle

How does water cycle through an environment?

MATERIALS jar with lid, soil, rocks or pebbles, sand, smaller containers, water, small plants, triple-beam balance

PROCEDURE

1 Construct an environment in a jar with a lid. You can use plants, soil, water, and containers.

2 Find the mass of your closed jar after you construct it.

3 Draw a detailed, colored picture of your jar.

4 Let your jar sit for several days.

5 Find the mass of your jar again, and draw another picture of it.

WHAT DO YOU THINK?

1. How did the jar's appearance change over several days?

_____

2. How did its mass change?

_____

3. What can you conclude about how water cycles through an environment?

_____

_____

CHALLENGE

How could you change your environment so that the jar's appearance would change at a faster rate?

_____

CHAPTER 11
The Water Planet

SECTION | DATASHEET
11.2 | Investigate Icebergs

Why do icebergs float?

MATERIALS balance, ice cube, 250 mL graduated cylinder, calculator; *for Challenge:* cork

PROCEDURE

❶ Find the masses of the empty graduated cylinder and the ice cube.

❷ Add 200 mL of water to the cylinder. Find the volume of the ice cube by measuring how much water it displaces. Make sure the water is extremely cold to prevent the ice cube from melting. Use the point of a paper clip to completely submerge the ice.

❸ Remove the water and let the ice melt in the cylinder.

❹ Calculate the density (density = mass/volume) of the ice cube. Now find the mass and volume of the liquid water from the melted ice and calculate its density.

OBSERVE AND ANALYZE

1. What was the density of the ice cube? the water?

_____

2. Why do icebergs float?

_____

_____

CHALLENGE

Float a cork in water. How does its behavior compare with that of floating ice?

_____

_____

_____

How can the ground filter water?

MATERIALS water, 1L plastic bottle with bottom cut off, pebbles, sand, soil, pepper, cocoa, food coloring, bottle bottom or bucket

PROCEDURE

1. Cap the top of the bottle. Invert it, and add to it a layer of gravel, then a layer of sand, then a layer of soil.

2. Slowly pour water onto the soil until a water table becomes visible in the sand beneath it.

3. Add the pollutants pepper, cocoa, and food coloring to the bottle top. Slowly unscrew the cap so that water trickles into the bucket.

4. Observe the water that filtered through.

5. Pour more water onto the soil and let water trickle out.

WHAT DO YOU THINK?

1. Which pollutants were filtered out before reaching the "aquifer"? Which ones reached the aquifer?

   _____

   _____

2. What effect does pollution have on drinking water that comes from aquifers?

   _____

   _____

CHALLENGE

What could you do to clean up an aquifer?

_____

_____

CHAPTER 11
The Water Planet

CHAPTER INVESTIGATION
Water Moving Underground

OVERVIEW AND PURPOSE

Many people rely on underground aquifers for their drinking water. Some aquifers are small and localized. Others can supply water to huge regions of the United States. Perhaps your own drinking water comes from an underground aquifer. In this investigation you will

- design an experiment to determine what types of materials best hold and transport water
- infer which types of Earth materials make the best aquifers

Problem

What types of materials will best hold and transport water?

Hypothesize

Write a hypothesis that answers the problem question in "If . . . , then . . . , because . . ." form.

_____

_____

MATERIALS

- granite sample
- sandstone sample
- sand
- square piece of cotton muslin or cotton knit, measuring 30 cm per side
- rubber band
- golf ball
- scale
- large jar
- water

Procedure

1 Design a procedure to test the materials samples to determine which will best hold and transport water. Your procedure should be designed to identify both which material absorbs the most water and which material absorbs water the fastest.

2 Record your procedure here.

_____

_____

_____

_____

_____

_____

3 Use the data table below to organize the data you will collect.

4 Be sure that you make both qualitative and quantitative observations.

5 Record your calculations here.

Observe and Analyze

1. **Record Observations** Draw a diagram of your experimental setup. .

[blank box]

2. **Calculate** Which item absorbed the most water?

_____

_____

3. **Scientific Method** How did you use the golf ball? What did it represent?

_____

_____

Conclude

1. **Interpret** Answer the problem question.

_____

_____

2. **Compare** Compare your results to your hypothesis. Do the results support your hypothesis?

_____

_____

3. **Identify Limits** In what ways was this activity limited in demonstrating how water moves underground? How might your experimental setup lead to incorrect conclusions?

_____

_____

_____

_____

4. **Apply** Look over your data table. Your results should indicate both which material absorbed the most water and which material absorbed water the fastest. How do these two characteristics compare in terms of their importance for an aquifer?

_____

_____

_____

5. **Infer** Which types of Earth materials make the best aquifers?

_____

_____

CHAPTER **11** | ADDITIONAL INVESTIGATION
Water Wells

OVERVIEW AND PURPOSE

You have learned that a water well is a hole in the ground that penetrates the water table. Also recall that in an artesian well, water flows upward without pumping as the result of pressure on the water. In this investigation you will

- make a model of an artesian well
- vary the angle of the model well to observe how this change affects water flow

Problem

Why does water flow from an artesian well?

Hypothesis

Think about what you know about artesian wells. Use this information to write a hypothesis to suggest why water flows from an artesian well without pumping. Write your hypothesis as an "If . . . , then . . . , because" statement.

_____

_____

_____

MATERIALS
- scissors
- tap water
- protractor
- metric ruler
- masking tape
- 250-mL beaker
- paper towels or rags
- funnel with narrow tip
- fine-lined permanent marker
- clear, oblong plastic storage box
- 30-cm piece of clear rubber tubing

TIME
45 minutes

Procedure

1 Work with a partner. Use the metric ruler and permanent marker to mark off a distance of 2 cm from one end of the plastic tubing.

2 Carefully use the scissors to cut a 3-mm hole into the tubing at the 2-cm mark, as shown below.

3 Close off the end of the tubing closest to the 2-cm mark with masking tape. Tape the tubing so that water will not escape, but do not use too much tape.

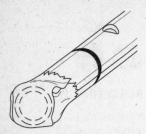

4 Carefully use the scissors to cut the top 2 cm from the tubing. Make the cut, as shown below.

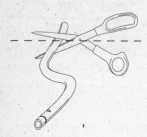

5 Gently push the end of the funnel into the top of the tubing.

6 Have your partner fill the beaker with tap water and wipe off any water from the outside of the beaker.

7 Use the protractor to position the tubing in the box, as shown below.

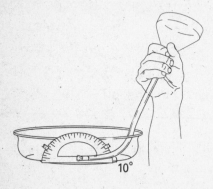

10°

8 Have your partner pour the water at a steady rate into the funnel without spilling any water onto the tubing. Keep the funnel nearly full, but do not let it overflow.

9 Observe what happens at the 3-mm hole. Record your observations in Table 1.

10 Pour the water that collects in the storage box in the container designated by your teacher. Drain the water from the tubing.

11 Dry off the tubing and the funnel.

12 Repeat steps 8–11, but change the angle of the model well to 20°.

13 Repeat step 12 for each of the other angles given in Table 1.

TABLE 1. HOW ANGLE AFFECTS WATER FLOW FROM AN ARTESIAN WELL	
Angle of Well in Relation to Bottom of Storage Box	Observations of Water Flow
10°	
20°	
30°	
40°	
50°	
60°	

Observe and Analyze

1. **Making Models** What part of your setup represents an aquifer?

   _____

2. **Explain** Explain what the walls of the rubber tubing in your setup represent.

   _____

   _____

3. **Making Models** What is the purpose of the funnel in this investigation?

   _____

   _____

4. **Compare** At which angle did the water flow from the 3 mm opening with the least pressure? the greatest pressure?

   _____

   _____

Conclude

1. **Conclude** Why did the water from the 60° well flow with more pressure than the water from the other wells?

   _____

   _____

   _____

2. **Explain** Explain why water flows from an artesian well.

   _____

   _____

   _____

DATASHEET
How Much Water Do You Use in a Week?

Showers	Multiply the number of minutes for the shower by 12 liters. Do the same for any additional showers and add them up. Enter number in the box.	
Baths	For a half tub, use 72 liters. For a full tub, 120 liters. Add up additional baths and enter the number.	
Toilets	Count the number of daily flushes. Multiply by 14 liters.	
Brushing teeth	For each time you brush your teeth, multiply by 12 liters (the number of liters used while the faucet runs for 1 minute).	
Hand washing	For each time you wash your hands, count the number of minutes you run the water. Multiply the number of minutes by 12 liters	
Drinking	Estimate how many liters of water and other liquids, such as milk, juice, and soda, you drink each day. Enter the number in the box.	
Household use	This number represents an estimate of your share of water used for water used for such purposes as laundry and dishwashing. For dishwashing, assume your share is 12 liters per day. For laundry, assume your share is 40 liters per day. Add these figures and enter the number in the box.	
Outdoor	Does your household use water outside? If so, estimate the number of minutes a hose is turned on each day. As an estimate of your share, multiply the number by 6 liters.	
Other uses	If you can think of any ways you use water, enter the number of liters in the box.	
Total	Add up the numbers in the box. This is an estimate of the amount of water you use each day.	
Weekly use	Multiply the total by 7 to calculate weekly use, and enter the number. This will be an average number, depending on how often dishes and clothes are washed, along with other variables.	

12.1 | Investigate Water Usage

How much water do you use in a week?

MATERIALS Water Use sheet, calculator

PROCEDURE

❶ Write down all the ways you use water in a day. Start with the time you get up in the morning. Include things such as brushing your teeth, flushing the toilet, using ice, and taking a shower.

❷ Look at the Water Use sheet, and from it, identify other ways that you and others in your household use water.

❸ Add up how many liters of water you use in a day, and multiply that by 7. This is how much water you use in a week.

WHAT DO YOU THINK?

1. Which of your activities used the most water?

   _____

   _____

2. What are some ways that you could reduce the amount of water you use weekly?

   _____

   _____

   _____

CHALLENGE

Based on your weekly water usage, how much water is used by the United States annually? Hint: Find the population of the United States in a reference source.

   _____

   _____

Investigate Water Conservation

How much water does a dripping faucet use?

MATERIALS water faucet, container, funnel, 100-mL graduated cylinder

PROCEDURE

❶ Adjust a faucet so that water drips slowly.

❷ Set a container under the faucet and collect the dripping water for five minutes.

❸ Turn off the faucet. Use the graduated cylinder to measure how much water dripped. Record your results in milliliters.

❹ Multiply the amount by 12 to determine how much water would drip in an hour. Then divide that number by 1000 to convert your result to liters.

WHAT DO YOU THINK?

1. How much water would one leaky faucet waste in a day?

_____

2. In a town with 2000 houses with one leaky faucet in each, how much water would be wasted each day?

_____

_____

CHALLENGE

How could you combine your results with those of your classmates to make the results more reliable?

_____

_____

CHAPTER
12 | CHAPTER INVESTIGATION
Monitoring Water Quality

OVERVIEW AND PURPOSE

Water pollution in some amount seems to happen wherever people live. That's why water for home drinking is almost always treated. Proper water treatment depends on knowing what forms of pollution water contains. This two-part activity models the process of monitoring for water quality. In this investigation you will

- perform systematic testing procedures similar to those used to test the water supply
- test known samples for common "pollutants," and then identify unknown water samples based on those tests

Procedure

MATERIALS

- 8 each of three types of indicator strips
- watch with second hand
- "pesticide-contaminated" water sample
- "bacteria-contaminated" water sample
- "chemical-contaminated" water sample
- pure distilled water sample
- 4 unknown water samples

PART 1

❶ Test the three different known contaminated water samples with the three types of indicator strips. Dip one of each strip into the solution and instantly remove it. A positive result causes a color change. Make your observations of color changes exactly 30 seconds after dipping the strip. Observe and note the results in Table 1 so you know what a positive result looks like for each contaminant. Do not reuse test strips. You need fresh strips for each water sample.

TABLE 1. POSITIVE TEST RESULTS OF KNOWN WATER SAMPLES				
	Pure Distilled Water	Chemical-Contaminated Water	Bacteria-Contaminated Water	Pesticide-Contaminated Water
Indicator A				
Indicator B				
Indicator C				

2 Test the pure distilled water with the three types of indicator strips, and note your results.

PART 2

1 A water-testing company has mixed up four water samples taken from the following locations: a runoff stream from an agricultural field, a river near a factory, a pond on a dairy farm, and a mountain stream. You will test the four unknown samples using the same procedures as above to determine which sample has which contaminant. You will then determine which location the sample most likely came from.

2 Test each water sample as in step 1, Part 1. Record in Table 2 your observations as you test each unknown sample with each indicator strip. Note all color changes you observe.

TABLE 2. TEST RESULTS OF UNKNOWN SAMPLES WITH PROBABLE LOCATIONS				
	Unknown #1	Unknown #2	Unknown #3	Unknown #4
Indicator A				
Indicator B				
Indicator C				
Type of Contaminant				
Location				

3 Consult Table 1 as you perform tests to determine which type of contaminant each unknown sample contains. From this information, determine which location the sample probably came from.

Observe and Analyze

1. Identify Controls Why was it necessary to test the distilled water in Part 1?

_____

_____

2. Identify Use what you have learned in this chapter to determine which location corresponds to the types of pollution you learned to identify in Part 1.

Pollutant	Location
Pesticide-Contaminated Water	
Bacteria-Contaminated Water	
Chemical-Contaminated Water	

3. Analyze Compare your testing results from the unknown water samples with your testing results from the known water samples. Are your results similar?

_____

_____

Conclude

1. Compare How did your results in Part 1 compare with your results in Part 2?

_____

_____

2. Evaluate What part of this investigation was the most difficult? Why?

_____

_____

3. **Identify Limits** What limitations does this type of testing pose for real-life water-quality technicians?

_____

_____

4. **Apply** A runoff pool is contaminated with bacteria, chemicals, and pesticides. How would your water-testing results appear for a sample from this pool?

_____

_____

CHAPTER 12 | ADDITIONAL INVESTIGATION
Desalination

OVERVIEW AND PURPOSE

People use fresh water for many things—drinking, cooking, bathing, and cleaning, just to name a few. Earth's supply of fresh water is limited. In some parts of the world, salt is removed from ocean water to provide fresh water. This process of removing salt from ocean water is called desalination. In this investigation you will

- make salt water
- experiment to desalinate your salt water

Problem

How can fresh water be obtained from salt water?

Hypothesize

Read the procedure. Based on the steps in this investigation, form a hypothesis to explain how you think fresh water can be obtained from salt water. Write your hypothesis as an "If . . . , then . . . , because" statement.

_____

_____

_____

MATERIALS
- small raw egg (in shell)
- tap water
- 125 g table salt
- 800-mL glass beaker
- 400-mL glass beaker
- stirring rod
- hot plate
- large metal spoon
- laboratory tongs
- graduated cylinder
- paper towels
- small weight to hold small beaker in place
- large glass funnel that completely covers the mouth of the large beaker
- cork for the large funnel

TIME
45 minutes

Procedure

1. Make the saltwater solution in the large beaker. Add the table salt to 500 mL of tap water. Stir the solution with the stirring rod until all of the salt is completely dissolved.

2. Test the relative density of the solution by carefully placing the raw egg onto the large spoon. Slowly lower the egg into the solution. A raw egg will float in salt water and sink in fresh water.

3. Use the large spoon to remove the egg from the salt water. Rinse the egg well with tap water. Use the paper towels to dry the egg completely. Leave the egg on the paper towels so that it cannot roll around.

4. Put the large beaker of salt water onto the hot plate.

5. Put the weight into the small beaker. Use the tongs to carefully lower the small beaker into the salt water. Do not let any of the salt water seep into the small beaker.

CHAPTER 12
Freshwater Resources

6 Put the cork into the spout of the funnel. Put the funnel over the large beaker. Make sure the funnel sits completely over the mouth of the large beaker.

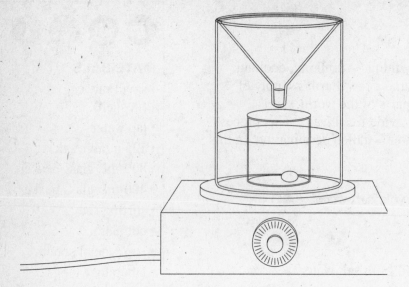

7 After you have gotten your teacher's approval, turn the hot plate on high. **CAUTION:** Always use care when working with any type of heat source.

8 Once the salt water begins to boil, observe your setup closely. In Table 1, record your observations of different parts of the setup.

9 When the salt water is nearly gone, turn off the hot plate. Wait at least 10 minutes for the beakers to cool.

10 Use tongs to remove the funnel from the top of the large beaker. Put the funnel aside.

11 Use the tongs to remove the small beaker from the setup. Put this beaker on the tabletop.

12 Use the tongs to remove the weight from the small beaker.

13 Test the relative density of the water in the small beaker by using the spoon to lower the egg into the water. Remember that a raw egg will float in salt water and sink in fresh water.

TABLE 1. DESALINATION OBSERVATIONS

Equipment	Observations
Funnel	
Small beaker	
Large beaker	

Observe and Analyze

1. **Observe** What happened to the egg in step 2?

   _____

   _____

2. **Communicate** What water-cycle process took place when the salt water boiled?

   _____

3. **Communicate** What water-cycle process took place on the inverted funnel?

   _____

4. **Infer** How do you know which type of water—salt or fresh—collected in the small beaker?

   _____

   _____

5. **Observe** Look at the large beaker. Describe its contents.

   _____

   _____

CHAPTER 12
Freshwater Resources

Conclude

1. **Draw Conclusions** What two processes resulted in the production of fresh water from salt water in this investigation?

   _____

2. **Communicate** Explain these processes in terms of changes in temperature and states of matter.

   _____

   _____

   _____

3. **Classify** There are two basic methods of desalination. One method uses a filter to strain salt from ocean water. This method is called reverse osmosis. The other method involves heating and evaporating salt water until it turns to vapor. This method is called distillation. Which method did you use in this investigation?

   _____

4. **Infer** Few desalination plants exist today in the United States because of the costs of removing salts from ocean water. In the future, desalination might be the only way for areas to get much-needed fresh water. Where in the United States do you think desalination of ocean water would be most cost-effective?

   _____

   _____

5. **Synthesize** How might desalination plants pollute nearby water environments?

   _____

   _____

   _____

SECTION | DATASHEET
13.1 | Investigate Density

How does dense water move?

MATERIALS 2 baby food jars, blue and red food coloring, tap water, 10 percent salt solution, index cards, large pan or bucket

PROCEDURE

❶ Read the instructions below and predict what will happen in steps 3 and 4 before you begin. Record your predictions.

_____

❷ Fill one jar with tap water and color it blue. Fill another jar with salt water and color it red. Place an index card over the top of the jar of red salt water.

❸ With your hand over the index card, turn the jar over and place it on top of the jar with the blue tap water. Pull out the index card and observe the water movement, if any.

❹ Repeat steps 2 and 3, but with the blue tap water on the top.

WHAT DO YOU THINK?

1. Describe any ways in which your observations differed from your predictions. On what did you base your predictions?

_____

_____

2. Explain why the water moved, if it did, in each of the two setups.

_____

_____

CHALLENGE

How do you think water in the ocean might be layered?

_____

_____

SECTION | DATASHEET
13.2 | Investigate Currents

What happens where bodies of water meet?

MATERIALS clear plastic box, aluminum foil, masking tape, high-salinity water, low-salinity water, pepper, sharp pencil

PROCEDURE

❶ Divide the box into two compartments, using masking tape and aluminum foil.

❷ Pour one solution into one side of the box while a partner pours the other solution into the opposite side. Be sure you and your partner pour at the same time in order to keep the barrier from breaking.

❸ Sprinkle pepper on the high-salinity side.

❹ Use the pencil to poke two holes in the aluminum foil—one just below the water surface and another near the bottom of the box. Observe for 10 minutes.

WHAT DO YOU THINK?

1. What did you observe in the box? Did you expect this?

_____

_____

2. What forces drove any movements of water you observed?

_____

CHALLENGE

Compare what you observed with what you have learned about the actual movements of water in the ocean. How could you change the experiment to better model actual ocean currents?

_____

_____

_____

_____

SECTION
13.4 | DATASHEET
Tides

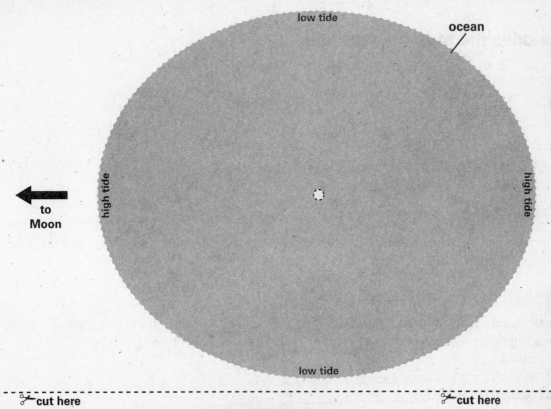

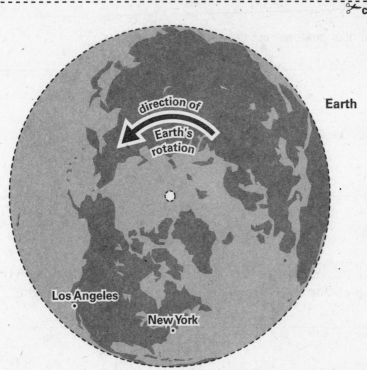

SECTION | DATASHEET
13.4 | **Investigate Tides**

CHAPTER 13
Ocean Systems

How does the Moon make tides?

MATERIALS Tides datasheet, scissors, brass paper fastener

PROCEDURE

1 Cut the Tides datasheet in two, along the dotted line. Cut out the map of Earth on the bottom half of the sheet.

2 Use a paper fastener to connect the two pieces.

3 Now you are ready to model the tides. Rotate Earth one full turn in the direction of the arrow. One full turn is equal to one day.

WHAT DO YOU THINK?

1. How does the model demonstrate the Moon's role in tides?

_____

_____

2. How many times does each place in the ocean experience high tide and low tide each day?

_____

_____

CHALLENGE

One full rotation of Earth takes place in a day, or 24 hours. About how much time passes between one high tide and the next high tide at any location on Earth?

_____

CHAPTER | CHAPTER INVESTIGATION
13 | **Wave Movement**

OVERVIEW AND PURPOSE

The particles in liquid water are constantly moving. Surfers, boaters, and people in inner tubes enjoy the effects of this motion—even though they never see what is happening at the particle level. How do water particles move in waves? In this investigation you will

- observe the movements of a floating object as waves pass through water
- use your observations to draw conclusions about how water particles move in waves

MATERIALS

- small aquarium or clear, shoebox-size container
- water
- small plastic dropping bottle or plastic spice container, with cap
- salt

Problem

What does the motion of a floating object reveal about the movement of water particles in a passing wave?

Hypothesize

Write a hypothesis to explain what the motion of a floating object might reveal about how water particles move in a wave. Your hypothesis should take the form of an "If . . . , then . . . , because . . ." statement.

_____

_____

Procedure

1. Fill the aquarium or clear container with cold tap water until it is three-quarters full.

2 Make the small bottle float with its top just below the surface of the water. You can accomplish this in several ways. First, try adding warm water to the bottle, then securely capping it without air bubbles. See if it will float. You can add salt to the bottle to move the bottle lower in the water. If the bottle is too low, you can trap a small air bubble under the cap to move the bottle higher in the water. Adjust these factors until you successfully float the bottle. The investigation will also work if the top of the bottle just touches the water's surface.

3 Remove the bottle from the water. Make sure the cap is tightly sealed.

4 Push your hand back and forth in the water at one end of the aquarium for about 30 seconds, to produce waves.

5 Gently place the small bottle back into the center of the aquarium. With your eyes level with the water surface, observe the motion of the waves and the bottle. Repeat as many times as needed until you notice the bottle behaving the same way with each passing wave.

Observe and Analyze

1. **Record** Make a diagram showing the aquarium setup, including the water, the waves, and the small bottle. Use arrows to show how the bottle moved as waves passed. Or you may draw several diagrams of the aquarium, showing the bottle at different locations as waves passed. Label the various parts of the waves.

2. Analyze Did the bottle travel with the wave? Why or why not?

_____

_____

Conclude

1. Interpret Compare your results with your hypothesis. Do your data support your hypothesis?

_____

_____

_____

2. Interpret Answer the problem question.

_____

_____

_____

3. Infer What do your observations tell you about particle movement in waves? Did the results surprise you? Explain.

_____

_____

_____

4. Evaluate Why was it necessary to float the bottle just under the surface of the water rather than letting it float right on top?

_____

_____

_____

5. Identify Problems What problems, if any, did you encounter in carrying out the procedure?

_____

_____

_____

CHAPTER 13
Ocean Systems

6. **Identify Limits** In what ways was this experiment limited in showing particle movement? Identify possible sources of error.

_____

_____

_____

7. **Predict** How do you think particle motion in a wave with a tall wave height might differ from that in a wave with a short wave height?

_____

_____

_____

8. **Synthesize** In this lab you made waves with your hand. In the ocean, most waves are caused by wind. Earthquakes, landslides, and other events also cause waves in the ocean. What do earthquakes, landslides, wind, and your hand have in common that allows all of them to make waves?

_____

_____

_____

CHAPTER 3 | ADDITIONAL INVESTIGATION
Measuring Salinity

OVERVIEW AND PURPOSE

You have learned that ocean water contains many kinds of salts. The amount of salts, or salinity, varies from place to place. A hydrometer is an instrument that can be used to measure salinity. In this investigation you will

- make a simple hydrometer
- use the hydrometer to measure the salinity of different water samples

Problem

How can a hydrometer be used to measure salinity?

Hypothesize

Look at the hydrometer shown in step 5. Use this illustration and what you know about salinity to hypothesize how your hydrometer will be used to measure salinity.

_____

_____

_____

Procedure

MATERIALS
- scissors
- filter paper
- 5 or 6 small BBs
- modeling clay
- table salt (10 g)
- stirring rod
- laboratory balance
- laboratory spatula
- plastic drinking straw
- distilled water (approximately 125 mL)
- 100-mL graduated cylinder
- saltwater solutions provided by your teacher
- 5 fine-lined permanent marking pens (one black and four other colors)

TIME

45 minutes

1 Form the modeling clay into a small ball. Gently push one end of the drinking straw into the clay to seal that end of the straw.

2 Place two BBs into the open end of the straw. This is your hydrometer.

3 Pour 100 mL of distilled water into the graduated cylinder.

4 Place your hydrometer, clay end down, into the water in the cylinder. Your hydrometer should float in the water. If it sinks, remove the instrument from the water and repeat steps 1 and 2.

5 Only about an inch of your hydrometer should be above the water in the cylinder. If more than an inch is above the water line, add BBs, one at a time, to weight your instrument.

6 Put your hydrometer into the water. Use the black permanent marker to make a small dot on the straw that shows where the water comes into contact with the instrument. Remove the instrument without spilling any of the water from the cylinder. Make a thin line around the straw at this point, and label the line with a "0."

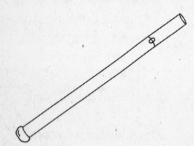

7 Use the balance to find the mass of a piece of filter paper.

Record that value here. _____

8 Use the spatula and balance to measure 1 g of the table salt onto the filter paper. Remember to subtract the mass of the paper from the total shown on the balance so that you have only 1 g of salt.

9 Add the salt to the graduated cylinder. Use the stirring rod to mix the solution until the salt is completely dissolved.

10 Carefully put your hydrometer back into the cylinder. Repeat Step 6, but label this line as "10."

11 Use the spatula and balance to measure another gram of the table salt onto the filter paper. Remember to subtract the mass of the paper from the total mass shown on the balance so that you have only 2 g of salt. Salinity is often expressed as the number of grams of salt per kilogram of water. This value is written as parts per thousand (ppt).

12 Repeat steps 9 and 10, but label this new line as "20."

13 Repeat steps 11–12 two more times, labeling the new lines as "30" and "40."

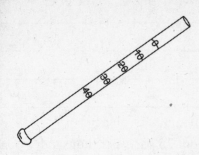

14 Get solution A from your teacher. Choose one of the colored markers to represent this sample. Record the color in the Table 1.

15 Pour 100 mL of solution A it into the empty graduated cylinder.

16 Put your hydrometer into the cylinder containing solution A. Repeat step 6, and mark the line in the color you have chosen for solution A. Estimate the salinity of solution A, and record it in Table 1.

17 Repeat steps 14–16 with solutions B, C, and D. Remember to choose and record a different color for each solution. Also remember to empty the cylinder before adding a new solution.

TABLE 1. SALINITY OF WATER SAMPLES	
Sample/Color	**Salinity**
A	
B	
C	
D	

Observe and Analyze

1. Measure What is the purpose of the "0" line?

_____

_____

_____

2. Sequence Rank the solutions provided by your teacher from the solution with the lowest salinity to the solution with the highest salinity. Explain how you arrived at your ranking.

_____

_____

_____

3. Explain Explain why you marked your instrument with the numbers *10, 20, 30,* and *40.*

_____

_____

_____

_____

4. Compare The salinity of actual ocean water ranges from about 25 parts per thousand to about 40 parts per thousand. How do the solutions in this investigation compare with this range?

_____

_____

_____

_____

Conclude

1. Generalize What factors can cause salinity to vary in Earth's oceans?

_____

_____

_____

2. Infer Which of the solutions tested might represent an area of ocean over which much rain falls? Explain.

_____

_____

_____

3. Infer Which of the solutions tested might represent an area of the ocean in which there is a high rate of evaporation? Explain.

_____

_____

_____

4. Conclude How might changes in salinity affect ocean organisms?

_____

_____

_____

SECTION DATASHEET
14.1 Investigate Coastal Environments

How do mussels survive?

MATERIALS small plastic containers with lids, sponges, water

PROCEDURE

1 Using the materials listed, design an experiment to demonstrate why mussels close their shells during low tide.

2 Write up your procedure.

_____

_____

_____

_____

_____

3 Test your experiment.

WHAT DO YOU THINK?

1. How does your experiment demonstrate why mussels close their shells?

_____

_____

_____

2. What were the variables in your experiment?

_____

CHALLENGE

How could you redesign your experiment to better model what happens during low tide? What other variables would you include?

_____

CHAPTER 14
Ocean Environments

SECTION
14.2 | DATASHEET
Investigate Floating

How do plankton float?

MATERIALS clear container, water, modeling clay, watch with a second hand

PROCEDURE

❶ Fill the clear container with tap water.

❷ Use the clay to make several different shapes that you think will stay afloat.

❸ One by one, place your clay models on the surface of the water. Time how long each piece takes to reach the bottom. Record your observations.

_____

_____

_____

WHAT DO YOU THINK?

1. What were the characteristics of the clay shape that sank the slowest?

_____

2. What factors affected how fast your clay shape sunk?

_____

_____

CHALLENGE

Some kinds of floating organisms release oil droplets or air bubbles to help them stay afloat. How could oil or air help them float?

_____

_____

_____

CHAPTER | CHAPTER INVESTIGATION
14 | Population Sampling

OVERVIEW AND PURPOSE

Scientists have found that overfishing is decreasing the
population of many organisms. They have also found that the
population of some other organisms are increasing. How do
scientists know this? They count the number of individuals
in a small measured area, called a quadrat, then estimate
from their counts how many organisms live in a larger area.
Repeated samplings over time allow them to determine whether
populations are growing or decreasing. In this investigation
you will

- count the number of items in a "population," using a
  quadrat technique
- use small and large quadrats to form two different
  estimates for the size of a "population"

MATERIALS
- calculator
- removable tape

Procedure

1. As a class, brainstorm some items that you might find in your classroom—for
   example: pencil, protractor, calculator, or ball cap. Choose one of those items to
   count. You will estimate the population at your school of this item.

2. Remove all of the items that your class decided to count from bags and drawers.
   For example, if your class is counting pencils, all students should remove all of
   their pencils and place them on their desks.

3. Divide your classroom into four equal-sized pieces. Use the tape to mark the
   boundaries of each quadrat. Label the quadrats A, B, C, and D.

CHAPTER 14
Ocean Environments

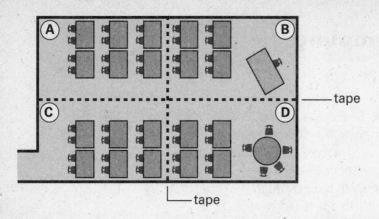

4 Count the items in one of the quadrats—A, B, C, or D. Record the number of items in Table 1.

TABLE 1. POPULATION DATA			
Quadrat	Number of Items	Classroom Population Estimate	School Population Estimate (number in classroom • number of classrooms in school)
A	7	$7 \cdot 4 = 28$	
B			
C			
D			
Total Classroom Count			

5 Find the total classroom population of your item by combining your data with the data from groups who counted other quadrats. Record the total classroom population in Table 1.

Observe and Analyze

1. **Calculate** Multiply the number of each item you counted in your quadrat by 4. This will give you an estimate of the number of each item in your classroom. Record your answer.

2. **Calculate** For this investigation, assume that each classroom in your school is the same size as your classroom. Your teacher will provide you with the number of classrooms in your entire school. Multiply your answer from question 1 by the number of classrooms in your school. This will give you an estimate of the number of each item in your school. Record your answer.

3. **Calculate** Now estimate the population of the items in the entire school, using the total count from the classroom. Multiply the total classroom population by the number of classrooms in your school. This will give you a second estimate for the population of each item in your school. Record your answer.

4. **Record** Make sure Table 1 is complete.

Conclude

1. **Compare** How does your school population estimate based on your small quadrat compare with your school population estimate based on your total classroom estimate?

_____

_____

2. **Infer** If there was a difference between your two total population estimates, what do you think could explain the difference?

_____

_____

3. **Infer** Do you think your total population estimate for your item in the school is accurate? Explain.

_____

_____

4. **Compare** How would your population estimate compare to one done the same way ten years ago? Ten years from now? Explain your reasoning.

_____

_____

5. **Identify Limits** What possible limitations or sources of error could have affected your results?

_____

_____

6. **Connect** How would you need to change your procedure if you were sampling an ocean fish population? Give at least two examples.

_____

_____

CHAPTER | ADDITIONAL INVESTIGATION
14 | **Oxygen in Ocean Water**

OVERVIEW AND PURPOSE

Oxygen is important for all living things, including the fish and millions of other organisms that live in Earth's oceans. The amount of oxygen dissolved in water depends on the pressure, temperature, and salinity of water and the activity of organisms. In this investigation you will use what you have learned about ocean environments to:

- make several samples of "ocean water," each with a different salinity
- test the water samples to compare the amount of dissolved oxygen in each

MATERIALS
- double pan balance
- filter paper
- table salt
- hot plate
- clock or watch
- four 250-mL glass beakers
- 4 thermometers
- stirring rod
- graduated cylinder
- glass marking pen
- laboratory spatula
- laboratory tongs
- tap water at room temperature

TIME
45 minutes

Problem

How does salinity affect the amount of oxygen dissolved in ocean water?

Hypothesize

Use the information above to form a hypothesis about how you think salinity might affect the amount of oxygen dissolved in ocean water. Your hypothesis should take the form of an "If . . . , then . . . , because . . ." statement.

_____

_____

_____

Procedure

❶ Label the beakers as follows: *Sample 1, Sample 2, Sample 3,* and *Sample 4.*

❷ Put 200 mL of the tap water into each beaker.

CHAPTER 14
Ocean Environments

3 Put the filter paper on the balance. Use the spatula to measure out 10 g of table salt.

4 Put the 10 g of salt into the beaker labeled *Sample 1*. Use the stirring rod to stir the mixture until all of the salt has completely dissolved.

5 Put the filter paper on the balance again. Use the spatula to measure out 20 g of salt.

6 Put the 20 g of salt into the beaker labeled *Sample 2*. Use the stirring rod to stir the mixture until all of the salt has completely dissolved.

7 Repeat steps 5 and 6, two more times. Each time, increase the mass of the salt by 10 grams. Make sure you put the appropriate amount of salt into the correct beaker. Check column 2 in Table 1 if necessary.

8 Put samples 1 and 2 on the hot plate. Insert a thermometer into each beaker.

9 Get your teacher's permission to turn the hot plate on low. Heat the water slowly so that the temperature increases by about 10° C per minute.

10 Just before the water starts to boil (about 90° C), observe the bubbles that form on the bottom of the beakers. Estimate the number of bubbles in each beaker and their approximate size in millimeters. Include your estimates in the "Observations" column of Table 1.

11 Use the tongs to remove the beakers from the hot plate. Put them aside to cool.

12 Repeat steps 8–11 for samples 3 and 4.

TABLE 1. OXYGEN VARIES WITH THE AMOUNT OF SALT IN THE WATER			
Sample	Amount of Salt in Sample	Observations of Sample as the Water Is Slowly Heated	Relative Amount of Dissolved Oxygen
1	10 g salt/ 200 mL water		
2	20 g salt/ 200 mL water		
3	30 g salt/ 200 mL water		
4	40 g salt/ 200 mL water		

Observe and Analyze

1. Identify Variables What was your independent variable in this investigation?

_____

_____

2. Identify Variables What was the dependent variable in this investigation?

_____

_____

3. Observe How did the size and number of bubbles vary among the water samples?

_____

_____

_____

_____

Conclude

1. Infer The dissolved oxygen in the water expanded as it became warmer, causing bubbles to form. As the water became warmer, the gas rose to the top of the beaker and escaped. Do you think that bubbles will form if you reheat the water in the beakers? Why or why not?

_____

_____

_____

_____

CHAPTER 14
Ocean Environments

2. **Infer** Based on your observations, how do you think the amount of oxygen dissolved in ocean water is affected by salinity?

_____

_____

_____

_____

3. **Compare** A lagoon is part of an ocean that is separated from the open ocean by a piece of land. The salinity of a lagoon is greater than the average salinity in the open ocean. How do you think the amount of dissolved oxygen in a lagoon compares with the oxygen contained in water farther from shore?

_____

_____

_____

_____

4. **Explain** How might the dissolved oxygen in ocean water vary with the seasons?

_____

_____

_____

_____

5. **Predict** How might a change in salinity in an area of the ocean affect the organisms that live there?

_____

_____

_____

_____

SECTION | DATASHEET
15.1 | Investigate Gas in the Air

How do you know that air has different gases?

MATERIALS limewater, 2 jars, spoon

PROCEDURE

1 Put a spoonful of limewater into each jar. Limewater is clear, but turns milky in the presence of carbon dioxide.

2 Cover one jar. Add extra carbon dioxide to the second jar by exhaling gently into it before you cover it. Tighten the lids carefully to seal the jars.

3 Predict what will happen, then shake each jar.

WHAT DO YOU THINK?

1. What happened to the limewater in each jar?

    _____

    _____

2. How do you know that air is made of different gases?

    _____

    _____

CHALLENGE

How would you test a different gas in the air?

_____

_____

_____

CHAPTER 15
Earth's Changing Atmosphere

SECTION
DATASHEET
15.2 | Investigate Solar Radiation

How does reflection affect temperature?

MATERIALS 2 cups, plastic wrap, white paper, tape, 2 short thermometers, a watch

PROCEDURE

1 Cover the top of one cup with plastic wrap. Cover the second cup with paper. Secure the plastic wrap and paper with tape.

2 Poke a small slit in each cup's cover. Insert a thermometer through each slit.

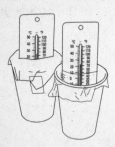

3 Place the cups in direct sunlight. Record their temperature every minute for 15 minutes.

WHAT DO YOU THINK?

How did the temperature change inside each cup?

_____

_____

How did the coverings contribute to these changes?

_____

_____

_____

_____

CHALLENGE

What does the paper represent in this model?

_____

_____

SECTION

15.3 | DATASHEET
Investigate Greenhouse Gases

How have levels of greenhouse gases changed?

MATERIALS CO_2 table sheet, graph sheet, regular pencil, red pencil

PROCEDURE

1 Plot the data for CO_2 levels on the graph sheet, using a regular pencil. Draw line segments to connect the points.

2 Plot the temperatures on the same graph, using a red pencil. Draw red line segments to connect the points.

INTERPRET DATA

How many times during the past 400,000 years were average temperatures in Antarctica above $-56°C$?

_____

_____

Do these changes seem to be connected to changes in carbon dioxide? Explain.

_____

_____

CHALLENGE

Is it possible to tell from the graph whether temperature affected carbon dioxide levels or carbon dioxide levels affected temperature? Why or why not?

_____

_____

_____

_____

CHAPTER 15
Earth's Changing Atmosphere

Name _____   Period _____   Date _____

SECTION 15.3 | DATASHEET
CO₂ Table Sheet

Graph the data below:

Time (thousand years before present)	CO₂ level (parts per million)	Temperature (°C)
400	279	−55.3
360	210	−60.6
320	272	−54.8
280	221	−60.8
240	214	−60.8
200	240	−57.9
160	193	−62.2
120	264	−54.8
80	226	−59.1
40	201	−61.2
0	280	−55.0

Carbon Dioxide and Temperature—Antarctica

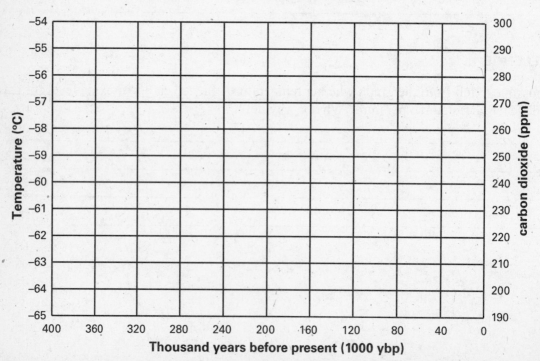

CHAPTER 15
Earth's Changing Atmosphere

CHAPTER 15 | CHAPTER INVESTIGATION
Observing Particulates

OVERVIEW AND PURPOSE

Many of us go through life unaware of particulates in the air, but allergy or asthma sufferers may become uncomfortably aware of high particulate levels. Certain particles, such as dust mite casings, can trigger asthma attacks. Particles that cling to surfaces can make them look dirty or even damage them. Some colors of surfaces may hide the dirt. In this investigation, you will

- compare the number and types of particles that settle to surfaces in two locations
- learn a method of counting particles

Problem

How do the types and numbers of particles in two different locations compare?

Hypothesize

You should decide on the locations in step 3 before writing your hypothesis. Write a hypothesis to explain how particulates collected at two different locations might differ. Your hypothesis should take the form of an "If …, then …, because …" statement.

_____

_____

MATERIALS
- 2 index cards
- ruler
- scissors
- transparent packing tape
- magnifying glass
- white paper
- black paper
- graph paper
- calculator

Procedure

1 Use the ruler to mark on each index card a centered square that is 3 cm per side. Carefully cut out each square.

2 On each card, place a piece of tape so that it covers the hole. Press the edges of the tape to the card, but do not let the center of the tape stick to anything. You should have a clean sticky window when you turn the card over.

3 Choose two different collecting locations where you can safely leave your cards—sticky side up—undisturbed overnight. You might place them on outside and inside window sills, on the ground and in a tree, or in different rooms.

4 Mark each card with your name, the date, and the location. Tape the cards in place so they will not blow away. Write your hypothesis. Collect your cards the next day.

Observe and Analyze

1. **Observe** Use the magnifying glass to inspect each card closely. Can you identify any of the particles? Try using white or black paper behind the card to help you see dark and light particles better. Describe and draw the types of particles from each card in the boxes below.

Location 1		Location 2	
White Background	**Black Background**	**White Background**	**Black Background**

How does the background affect the type or number of particles you see?

_____

_____

2. **Record** Place each card onto a piece of graph paper. Line up the top and left edges of each card's center square with the grid on the graph paper and tape the card down. Choose four graph-paper squares and count the number of visible particles in each square. Use the magnifying glass. Record your results in the data table.

	Number of particles						Notes
	Sq. 1	Sq. 2	Sq. 3	Sq. 4	Ave./sq.	Ave./cm^2	
Card 1							
Card 2							

3. Calculate Average Calculate the average number of particles per square for each card.

$$\text{average} = \frac{\text{sum of particles in 4 squares}}{4}$$

Location 1

_____
_____
_____
+ _____
_____
_____ ÷ 4 = _____

Location 2

_____
_____
_____
+ _____
_____
_____ ÷ 4 = _____

Convert Use the formula below to convert from particles per square to particles per square centimeter. If your squares were half a centimeter wide, then use 0.5 cm in the denominator below.

$$\text{particles per } cm^2 = \text{particles per square} = \frac{1 \text{ square}}{(\text{width (in cm) of square})^2}$$

Use the space below to do your calculations. First, square the width to get cm^2, then divide 1 square by the result.

Multiply your answer by the particles per square to get the particles per cm^2.

Location 1

Location 2

CHAPTER 15
Earth's Changing Atmosphere

Conclude

1. **Compare** Compare the types of particles found on each card. List similarities and differences. Compare the numbers of particles found on the cards.

_____

_____

_____

2. **Interpret** Compare your results with your hypothesis. Do your data support your hypothesis?

_____

_____

3. **Infer** What can you infer about where the particles came from or how they reached each location? What evidence did you find to support these inferences?

_____

_____

_____

4. **Identify Limits** What possible limitations or sources of error might have affected your results? Why was it necessary to average the number of particles from several squares?

_____

_____

_____

5. **Evaluate** Do you think the color of the graph paper affected the number of particles you were able to count?

_____

_____

6. **Apply** What color would you choose for playground equipment in your area? Explain your choice.

_____

_____

_____

_____

CHAPTER **15** | ADDITIONAL INVESTIGATION
Oxygen in the Air

OVERVIEW AND PURPOSE

You have learned that most of the materials in Earth's atmosphere are gases. Recall, too, that the two most common gases in the air are nitrogen and oxygen. In this investigation you will

- observe the oxidation of a piece of steel wool in a test tube
- use the test tube containing the steel wool to determine the percent of oxygen that was present in the air in the test tube

Problem

How can you measure the percent of oxygen in the air?

Hypothesize

Use the information in the **Overview and Purpose** and the illustration of the setup in your textbook to form a hypothesis to explain what will happen in the test tube that contains the steel wool. Your hypothesis should be written as an "If . . . , then, . . . , because . . . " statement.

MATERIALS

- 2 identical test tubes
- transparent metric ruler with millimeter markings
- plastic gloves
- scissors
- soapless steel-wool pad
- laboratory stirring rod
- fine-lined, permanent marking pen
- large graduated cylinder
- water
- 2 identical beakers (500 mL)
- laboratory ringstand
- 2 test-tube clamps

TIME: 45 minutes

_____

Procedure

❶ Measure the length, in mm, of each test tube. Record the measurement in Data Table 1.

❷ Put on the gloves. Carefully use the scissors to cut a piece of steel wool about the size of a cherry tomato from the pad.

❸ Use the laboratory stirring rod to carefully push the piece of steel wool down to the bottom of one of the test tubes as shown below.

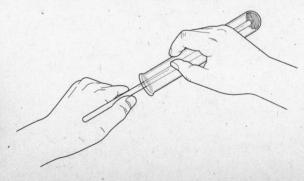

CHAPTER 15
Earth's Changing Atmosphere

④ Use the graduated cylinder to measure 25 mL of water.

⑤ Pour the water into the test tube containing the steel wool.

⑥ Put your thumb over the open end of the tube and shake the tube for about 20 seconds. Pour the water out.

⑦ Use the rod to check to see that the steel wool is still at the end of the test tube.

⑧ Repeat steps 4–6 for the empty test tube.

⑨ Use the graduated cylinder to measure 450 mL of water. Pour the water into one of the beakers.

⑩ Repeat step 9 for the other beaker.

⑪ Place the beakers on either side of the ringstand as shown.

⑫ Use the ruler to measure 10 mm from the open end of one of the test tubes. Mark this point with a fine-lined marking pen. Repeat for the other test tube.

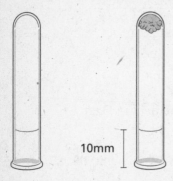

10mm

⑬ Secure one of the clamps to the empty test tube. Now secure the clamp to the ringstand so that the test tube is submerged to the mark you made with the pen.

14 Repeat step 13 for the test tube containing the steel wool. Make sure the water inside this test tube is at the position indicated by the marked line.

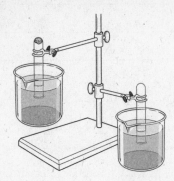

15 Use the metric ruler to measure the height of the water in each test tube. Record your measurements in the data table.

16 Continue to observe the test tubes for the next few days until the water no longer rises. Measure and record the final height of the water column in the table.

DATA TABLE 1: DETERMINING THE AMOUNT OF OXYGEN IN AIR					
	Length of Test Tube (mm)	Final Height of Water (mm)	Change in Height of Water (mm)	Percent Change in Air	Observations
Tube without steel wool					
Tube with steel wool					

Observe and Analyze

1. **Identify Variables** Why was it necessary to add add water to both test tubes?

_____

_____

_____

2. **Identify Limits** Why was the volume of air in the two test tubes different when you started this experiment?

_____

_____

3. **Describe** Describe any changes to the steel wool.

_____

_____

_____

4. **Compare and Contrast** How did the initial and final levels of water in the test tubes compare?

_____

_____

_____

5. **Calculate** Determine the change of the amount of air in the test tube. Do this by subtracting the initial height of the water in the test tube from the final height. This number is also the change in the height of air in the test tube. Do your calculations on a separate sheet of paper. Record your answer in the data table.

6. **Calculate** Calculate the percent of oxygen that was in the air. Subtract the initial height of water from the length of the test tube. This number is the initial amount of air in the test tube. Now divide the change in air by the initial amount of air. You will be dividing a smaller number by a larger number. Multiply your last number by 100%. Show your calculations on a separate sheet of paper.

_____

Conclude

1. **Explain** Explain why water moved up into the test tube containing the steel wool. **Hint:** Think about what happens during oxidation.

_____

_____

2. **Compare** How does your value of oxygen compare to the value given on page 11 in your textbook? Explain any differences.

_____

_____

_____

SECTION
16.1 DATASHEET

Investigate Air Pressure

How can you measure changes in air pressure?

MATERIALS scissors, round balloon, metal can, rubber band, thin straw, tape, ruler

PROCEDURE

1. Cut open a balloon along one side until you get close to the end. Stretch the balloon across the open top of the can. Secure it tightly in place with a rubber band.

2. Cut the straw on an angle to make a pointer. Tape the other end of the straw to the center of the balloon.

3. Tape a ruler against a wall or a box so that the end of the pointer almost touches the ruler. Record the position of the pointer against the ruler.

4. Record the position of the pointer at least once a day for the next five days. Look for small changes in its position. For each day, record the air pressure printed in a local newspaper.

WHAT DO YOU THINK?

1. In what direction did the pointer move when the air pressure went up? when the air pressure went down?

_____

_____

Explain how your instrument worked.

_____

_____

CHALLENGE

Predict what would happen to the pointer if you repeated this experiment but poked some small holes in the balloon.

_____

CHAPTER 16
Weather Patterns

SECTION DATASHEET
16.2 | Investigate the Coriolis Effect

How does Earth's rotation affect wind?

MATERIALS round balloon, felt-tip pen

PROCEDURE

1 Blow up a balloon and tie it off.

2 Have a classmate slowly rotate the balloon to the right. Draw a line straight down from the top of the balloon to the center as the balloon rotates.

3 Now draw a line from the bottom of the balloon straight up to the center as the balloon rotates.

WHAT DO YOU THINK?

1. How did the rotation affect the lines that you drew?

2. How does this activity demonstrate the Coriolis effect?

CHALLENGE

How might changing the speed at which the balloon is rotated affect your results? Repeat the activity to test your prediction.

CHAPTER 16
Weather Patterns

SECTION
16.3
DATASHEET
Investigate Condensation

How does a cloud form?

MATERIALS clear 1-liter plastic bottle with cap, water at room temperature, tablespoon, matches

PROCEDURE

1 Add a spoonful of water to the bottle to increase humidity inside it.

2 Lay the bottle on its side. Light a match, blow it out, and then stick the match into the bottle for a few seconds to let smoke flow in. Replace the cap.

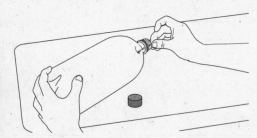

3 Squeeze the bottle quickly and then release it. Observe what happens when the bottle is allowed to expand.

WHAT DO YOU THINK?

1. What happened to the water vapor inside the bottle when you squeezed the bottle and then let it expand?

_____

2. How did the smoke affect what happened to the water vapor?

_____

CHALLENGE

How would the cloud change if you raised or lowered the temperature inside the bottle?

_____

_____

CHAPTER 16
Weather Patterns

How much rain falls during a storm?

MATERIALS scissors, 1-liter plastic bottle, gravel, water, permanent marker, ruler

PROCEDURE

1 Cut off the top third of the bottle. Set this part aside.

2 Put some gravel at the bottom of the bottle to keep it from tipping over. Add water to cover the gravel. Draw a horizontal line on the bottle at the top of the water. Use a ruler to mark off centimeters on the bottle above the line that you drew. Now take the part of the bottle that you set aside and turn it upside down. Fit it inside the bottle to create a funnel.

3 Place the bottle outside when a rainstorm is expected. Make sure that nothing will block rain from entering it. Check your rain gauge after 24 hours. Observe and record the rainfall.

WHAT DO YOU THINK?

1. How much rain fell during the time period?

_____

2. How do the measurements compare with your observations?

_____

_____

CHALLENGE

Do you think you would measure the same amount of rain if you used a wider rain gauge? Explain.

_____

_____

CHAPTER 16 | DATASHEET
Relative Humidity (%)

Dry-Bulb Temperature (°C)	0	1	2	3	4	5	6	7	8	9	10	11	12	13	14	15
−20	100	28														
−18	100	40														
−16	100	48														
−14	100	55	11													
−12	100	61	23													
−10	100	66	33													
−8	100	71	41	13												
−6	100	73	48	20												
−4	100	77	54	32	11											
−2	100	79	58	37	20	1										
0	100	81	63	45	28	11										
2	100	83	67	51	36	20	6									
4	100	85	70	56	42	27	14									
6	100	86	72	59	46	35	22	10								
8	100	87	74	62	51	39	28	17	6							
10	100	88	76	65	54	43	33	24	13	4						
12	100	88	78	67	57	48	38	28	19	10	2					
14	100	89	79	69	60	50	41	33	25	16	8	1				
16	100	90	80	71	62	54	45	37	29	21	14	7	1			
18	100	91	81	72	64	56	48	40	33	26	19	12	6			
20	100	91	82	74	66	58	51	44	36	30	23	17	11	5		
22	100	92	83	75	68	60	53	46	40	33	27	21	15	10	4	
24	100	92	84	76	69	62	55	49	42	36	30	25	20	14	9	4
26	100	92	85	77	70	64	57	51	45	39	34	28	23	18	13	9
28	100	93	86	78	71	65	59	53	47	42	36	31	26	21	17	12
30	100	93	86	79	72	66	61	55	49	44	39	34	29	25	20	16

CHAPTER 16
Weather Patterns

CHAPTER
16 | CHAPTER INVESTIGATION
Relative Humidity

OVERVIEW AND PURPOSE

Finding out the relative humidity can help you predict how comfortable you will feel on a hot day or whether dew will form on the ground. You can use a psychrometer to measure relative humidity. A psychrometer is a device made from two thermometers—one with a wet bulb and the other with a dry bulb. In this activity, you will

- make a milk-carton psychrometer
- use it to measure the relative humidity of the air at two locations in your school

Problem

Which location will have the greater relative humidity?

_____

MATERIALS
- 2 thermometers
- cotton or felt cloth
- 3 rubber bands
- plastic bowl
- water at room temperature
- scissors
- pint milk carton
- ruler
- Relative Humidity Chart

Hypothesize

Write a hypothesis in "if . . . , then . . . , because" form to answer the problem.

_____

Procedure

1 Check the two thermometers that you are using in this experiment to make sure they read the same temperature. Wrap a piece of cotton or felt cloth around the bulb of one thermometer. Hold the cloth in place with a rubber band as shown in the photograph below. Dip this wet-bulb thermometer into a bowl of room-temperature water until the cloth is soaked.

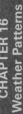

2 Use scissors to cut a small hole in one side of the milk carton, 2 centimeters (about 0.75 in.) from the bottom of the carton. Place the wet-bulb thermometer on the same side as the hole that you made in the milk carton, and attach it with a rubber band. Push the tail of the cloth through the hole as shown. Attach the other thermometer to the carton by slipping it under the two rubber bands holding the wet-bulb thermometer in place. This is the dry-bulb thermometer.

3 Fill the carton with water to just below the hole so that the cloth will remain wet. Empty the bowl and place the completed psychrometer inside it.

4 Write "science room" under the heading "Location 1" in the data table below. Take your first readings in the science classroom about 10 minutes after you set up your psychrometer. Read the temperatures on the two thermometers in degrees Celsius. Record the temperature readings for the first location in the first column of the data table.

DATA TABLE 16.1 RELATIVE HUMIDITY AT VARIOUS LOCATIONS		
	Location 1	**Location 2**
Dry-bulb temperature		
Wet-bulb temperature		
Subtract wet-bulb from dry-bulb reading		
Relative humidity		

5 Choose a second location in your school, and identify it under the heading "Location 2" in the data table. Take a second set of temperature readings with your psychrometer in this location. Record the readings in the second column of the data table.

6 Subtract the wet-bulb reading from the dry-bulb reading for each location. Record this information in the third row of the data table.

7 Use the relative humidity table your teacher provided to find each relative humidity (expressed as a percentage). In the left-hand column, find the dry-bulb reading for Location 1 that you recorded in step 5. Then find in the top line the number you recorded in Step 7 (the difference between the wet and dry-bulb readings). Move your finger down that column until you reach the ruler. Record the relative humidity in the last row of the data table. Repeat these steps for Location 2.

Observe and Analyze

1. **Record Observations** Draw the setup of your psychrometer in the box below. Be sure your data tables are complete.

2. **Identify** Identify the variables and constants in this experiment. List them in the data table below.

DATA TABLE 16.2	
Variables	Constants
1.	1.
2.	2.

3. **Compare** How do the wet-bulb readings compare with the dry-bulb readings?

_____

_____

_____

4. **Analyze** If the difference between the temperature readings on the two thermometers is large, is the relative humidity high or low? Explain why.

_____

_____

Conclude

1. **Interpret** Answer the question in the problem. Compare your results with your hypothesis.

_____

_____

_____

2. **Identify Limits** Describe any possible errors that you made in following the procedure.

_____

_____

_____

_____

3. **Apply** How would you account for the differences in relative humidity that you obtained for the two locations in your school?

_____

_____

_____

_____

CHAPTER 16 | ADDITIONAL INVESTIGATION
Estimating Wind Speed

OVERVIEW AND PURPOSE

You have learned that wind is the horizontal movement of air. The speed of this movement of air can be measured with an anemometer. In this investigation, you will

- make a simple cup anemometer.
- use the anemometer to estimate wind speed.

Problem

How does an anemometer measure wind speed?

Hypothesize

Read the Materials list and the Procedure for this investigation. Use this information to hypothesize how you can use these materials to make an instrument that measures wind speed.

_____

_____

_____

MATERIALS
- ruler
- stiff cardboard
- scissors
- push pin
- stapler
- 3 small clear plastic cups
- 1 small colored plastic cup
- modeling clay
- unsharpened pencil
- meter stick
- watch with second hand

TIME
45 minutes

PROCEDURE

1 Use the metric ruler and a pencil to mark the outlines of two strips of stiff cardboard, each 30 cm long and 5 cm wide. Use the scissors to carefully cut out the two strips.

2 Use the ruler to find the center of each strip of cardboard. Mark the center with a small point. Use the pin to make a small hole through the point on each strip.

3 Overlap the strips to form a plus sign (+). The small pin holes must be overlapping, and the strips must be perpendicular.

4 Staple the strips as shown below.

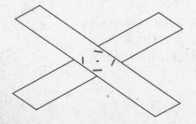

5 Use the stapler to attach the cups to the free ends of the cardboard strips as shown below. Make sure all of the open ends of the cups are facing the same direction.

6 Use the push pin to attach the strips to the unsharpened pencil's eraser. Push the pin into the center of the strips and into the eraser. Use the modeling clay to form a base for your instrument. Put the pencil with the strips and cups into the clay base.

7 Hold the pencil in one hand at arm's length from your body. Ask another student to blow gently into one of the cups. If your instrument doesn't spin freely, adjust the push pin.

8 Go outdoors on a day with medium-force winds. Find a flat area where the instrument won't be disturbed but will receive wind. Place the instrument on the ground.

9 Check to see that the top of the instrument spins freely. Adjust the pin, if necessary. Adjust the pencil so that it is vertical.

10 Stand next to your instrument so that the colored cup is in front of you. With a partner, use the second hand on the watch to count how many times the colored cup passes you in 60 seconds. Record this value in the data table.

11 Repeat steps 8–10 three more times in three different locations. Remember to place the instrument directly on the ground.

12 Now hold the instrument in your hand at arm's length and 1.5 meters above the ground. You can remove the pencil from the clay base to make it easier to hold. Make sure that the instrument is vertical. Record in your data table how many times the colored cup passes you in 60 seconds.

CHAPTER 16
Weather Patterns

🔞 Record wind speed measurements at the three other locations you chose. Keep the instrument 1.5 meters from the ground. Record your findings in your data table.

DATA TABLE: RELATIVE WIND "SPEED" MEASUREMENTS *			
Location	Time of Day	Relative Wind Speed on Ground (turns/minute)	Relative Wind Speed at 1.5 meters (turns/minute)
1.			
2.			
3.			
4.			

* Remember, your instrument can't measure actual wind speeds. It does, however, give you a relative wind speed.

Observe and Analyze

1. Explain Why did you have to find the center of the cardboard strips and the straws?

_____

_____

_____

2. Infer What would have happened if the pencil part of your anemometer wasn't vertical when you were making measurements?

_____

_____

_____

Conclude

1. Interpret Interpret the data in your table. How did wind speed differ in each of the locations?

_____

_____

2. Analyze What might have caused differences in wind speed at the different locations?

_____

_____

CHAPTER 16
Weather Patterns

3. **Compare** Compare the readings taken on the ground with readings taken at 1.5 meters above the ground. Describe any patterns in the data.

_____

_____

4. **Analyze** If you wanted to obtain accurate readings of wind speed for an area, where would you locate your instrument? Explain why.

_____

_____

_____

SECTION
17.1 | DATASHEET
Investigate Air Masses

What happens when air masses collide?

MATERIALS 500 mL beaker, stiff cardboard, scissors, 2 cups, small beaker for measuring, food coloring, salt, water

PROCEDURE

1 Cut the cardboard to create a snug barrier that divides your beaker in half.

2 Mix about 5 mL salt, 50 mL water, and a drop of blue food coloring in one cup. This dense mixture represents a cold air mass.

3 Mix 50 mL water with a drop of red food coloring in the other cup. This less-dense mixture represents a warm air mass.

4 Carefully pour the red water into one side of your divided beaker and the blue saltwater into the other side. As you look through the side of the beaker, quickly remove the barrier.

WHAT DO YOU THINK?

1. What happened when the two liquids met?

_____

_____

_____

2. To what extent did the liquids mix together?

_____

CHALLENGE

3. How are the liquids like air masses?

_____

_____

_____

SECTION | DATASHEET
17.2 | Investigate Ice

Why put salt on icy roads?

MATERIALS 2 ice cubes, 2 cups, table salt

PROCEDURE

1 Place one ice cube in each cup.

2 Sprinkle salt onto the top of one of the ice cubes and observe for several minutes.

WHAT DO YOU THINK?

1. Which ice cube melted first?

_____

2. Why do people put salt on roads in winter?

_____

CHALLENGE

3. Why do people put sand or cinders on icy roads? Design an experiment to test your ideas. Write a hypothesis and procedure. Record your results. Did your results support your hypothesis? Why or why not?

SECTION
17.3
DATASHEET
Investigate Updrafts

How do updrafts form?

MATERIALS clear container, 5 foam cups, 4 cardboard squares, food coloring, eyedropper, cool water, hot tap water

PROCEDURE

1 Set up the cardboard, the cups, the container, and the cool water as in the diagram. Wait for the water to become still.

2 Use the eyedropper to place 2-3 drops of coloring at the bottom of the water.

3 Slide a cup of hot water (about 70°) beneath the food coloring.

WHAT DO YOU THINK?

In what ways was the motion of the water like the air in a thunderstorm?

_____

_____

_____

CHALLENGE

How could you observe updrafts in air?

_____

_____

_____

_____

_____

CHAPTER | CHAPTER INVESTIGATION
17 | **Design a Weather Center**

OVERVIEW AND PURPOSE

The accuracy of a weather forecast depends largely on the type and quality of the data that it is based on. In this lab, you will use what you have learned about weather to

- observe and measure weather conditions
- record and analyze the weather-related data

MATERIALS
- thermometer
- magnetic compass
- other weather instruments
- graph paper

Procedure

1 Survey the possible sources of weather data in and around your classroom. You can use a thermometer to record the outside air temperature. You can observe cloud types and amount of cloud cover from a window or doorway. You can also observe precipitation and notice if it is heavy or light. If there is a flag in view, use it to find the wind direction and to estimate wind speed. Use the magnetic compass to determine the direction of north.

2 Assemble or make tools for your observations. You may want to make a reference chart with pictures of different cloud types or other information. Decide if you wish to use homemade weather instruments. You may have made a barometer, a psychrometer, and a rain gauge already. If not, see the instructions in your textbook. You may also wish to do research to learn how to make or use other weather instruments.

3 Make an initial set of observations. Write down the date and time. Record the readings from the thermometer and other instruments.

4 Decide how to record your observations of the clouds, wind, and any precipitation. Organize your notes to make it easy for you to record later observations in a consistent way.

_____

_____

_____

_____

_____

_____

_____

5 Create a chart with a row for each type of observation you are making. You might darken fractions of circles to record amounts of cloud cover, as shown in the station symbols in your textbook. Make sure each row has a heading and enough room for numbers, words, or sketches. Include a row for notes that do not belong in the data rows.

6 Record your observations every day at the same time. Try to make the observations exactly the same way each time. If you have to redraw your chart, copy the information carefully.

Observe and Analyze

1. **Graph** Graph the data you collect that represents measurable quantities. Use graphs that are appropriate to your data. Often a simple line graph will work. Choose an appropriate scale and interval based on the range of your data. Make the x-axis of each graph the same so that you can compare the different types of data easily. Draw your graphs on graph paper.

2. **Compare and Contrast** Look at your graphs for patterns in your data. Some aspects of weather change at the same time because they are related to each other. Did one type of change occur before a different type of change? If so, this may help you predict weather.

_____

_____

_____

Conclude

1. **Interpret** Did a front pass through your area during the period you observed? What observations helped you answer this question?

_____

_____

_____

2. **Evaluate** Why was it necessary to observe at the same time each day?

_____

_____

_____

3. **Apply** If you predicted that each day's weather would be repeated the next day, how often would you be right?

_____

_____

_____

CHAPTER 17 | ADDITIONAL INVESTIGATION
Hurricane Hugo

OVERVIEW AND PURPOSE

You've learned that a hurricane is a tropical low-pressure system that forms when energy from warm ocean water is released. In this investigation, you will use what you've learned about hurricanes to

- chart the movement of Hurricane Hugo through the Atlantic Ocean
- answer questions about the different stages of development of Hurricane Hugo

<table>
<tr><td>MATERIALS
• sharp pencil
• colored pencil
• copy of chart on next page
TIME
45 minutes</td></tr>
</table>

Problem

Read through the Procedure for this investigation. Study the data given in the table and note any patterns. Use the procedure and the data to answer these questions: When did the tropical storm become a hurricane? How did Hurricane Hugo move through the Atlantic Ocean? What happened when Hugo reached land?

Procedure

1 Plot the data directly onto the hurricane tracking chart on the following page. Mark the date and category at each point.

2 Use the data to plot the location of Hurricane Hugo on each of the days given in the data table. Recall that lines of latitude run have labels, such as 30°N, to indicate a distance north or south of the equator. Lines of longitude have labels, such as 40°W, to indicate a distance east or west of the prime meridian.

3 Use a regular pencil to connect the first five data points. Then, with a colored pencil, mark the data points where Hugo was a hurricane, and connect those points. Use a regular pencil to finish connecting the data points.

4 Use the chart you drew showing Hugo's path and the data in the table to answer the questions in the **OBSERVE AND ANALYZE** and **CONCLUDE** sections of this lab.

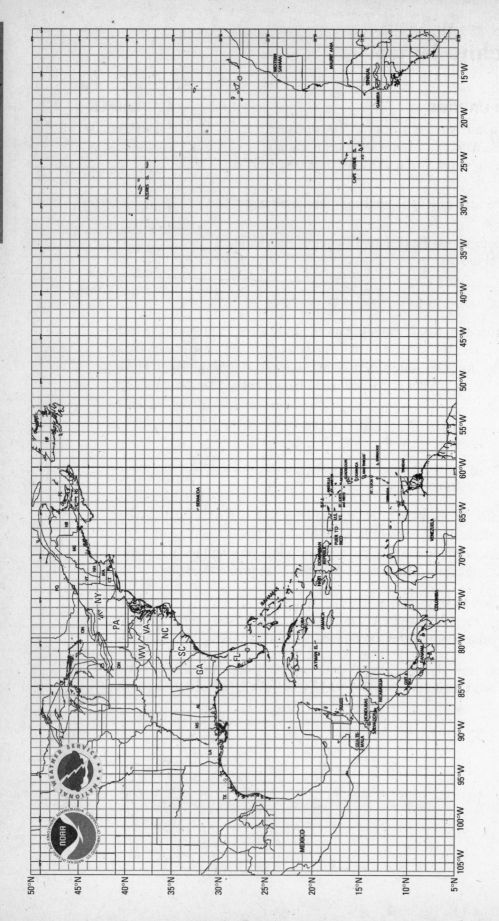

DATA TABLE HURRICANE HUGO STATISTICS				
Date	Time (z)	Latitude (°N)	Longitude (°W)	Storm Category
09/11/89	18	12.5°	29.2°	Tropical storm
09/12/89	6	12.5°	32.9°	Tropical storm
09/12/89	12	12.5°	34.8°	Tropical storm
09/12/89	18	12.6°	36.7°	Tropical storm
09/13/89	12	12.8°	41.8°	Tropical storm
09/13/89	18	12.8°	43.5°	Hurricane 1
09/14/89	12	13.2°	47.8°	Hurricane 2
09/14/89	18	13.6°	49.1°	Hurricane 2
09/15/89	6	14.0°	51.9°	Hurricane 3
09/15/89	12	14.2°	53.3°	Hurricane 4
09/15/89	18	14.6°	54.6°	Hurricane 5
09/16/89	0	15.4°	58.4°	Hurricane 4
09/16/89	18	15.8°	59.4°	Hurricane 4
09/17/89	12	16.6°	62.5°	Hurricane 4
09/17/89	18	16.9°	63.5°	Hurricane 4
09/18/89	12	18.2°	65.5°	Hurricane 3
09/18/89	18	19.1°	66.4°	Hurricane 3
09/19/89	6	20.7°	67.3°	Hurricane 2
09/19/89	12	21.6°	68.0°	Hurricane 2
09/20/89	6	24.4°	70.1°	Hurricane 2
09/20/89	12	25.2°	71.0°	Hurricane 2
09/21/89	6	28.0°	74.9°	Hurricane 3
09/21/89	18	30.2°	77.5°	Hurricane 4
09/22/89	6	33.5°	80.3°	Hurricane 2
09/22/89	12	35.9°	81.7°	Tropical storm
09/22/89	18	38.5°	81.8°	Tropical storm

* The Saffir-Simpson Hurricane Scale rates a hurricane from 1 to 5 depending on its intensity.

Category	Sustained Wind Speed
Hurricane 1	119–153 km/hr
Hurricane 2	154–177 km/hr
Hurricane 3	178–209 km/hr
Hurricane 4	210–249 km/hr
Hurricane 5	over 249 km/hr

Data show representative locations and events. Time is given as Zulu, also called Universal Time.

Observe and Analyze

1. **Analyze Data** When did the tropical storm develop into Hurricane Hugo?

   _____

2. **Interpret Data** When did Hugo reach its peak strength?

   _____

3. **Describe** Use your map to describe the path of Hurricane Hugo through the Atlantic Ocean basin.

   _____

   _____

4. **Analyze Data** Where was Hugo when it stopped being a hurricane and was classified as a tropical storm again?

   _____

Conclude

1. **Explain** Explain what caused the tropical storm on September 13 to develop into a hurricane.

   _____

   _____

2. **Synthesize** When and where did Hugo reach land? What happened to the storm at that point?

   _____

   _____

3. **Interpret** Does the path on your map show all the locations Hugo affected? Give your reasons.

   _____

   _____

   _____

   _____

SECTION
18.1 | DATASHEET
Investigate Heating and Cooling Rates

How quickly do soil and water heat and cool?

MATERIALS 2 cups, ruler, soil, water at room temperature, 2 thermometers, sunlight or lamp

PROCEDURE

❶ Mark a line 3 centimeters from the top of each cup. Fill one cup to the line with water and the other with soil. Place a thermometer into the contents of each cup. Wait 2 minutes. Record the temperature in each cup.

❷ Place the cups side by side in bright sunlight or under a lamp. Wait 10 minutes. Record the temperature in each cup.

❸ Move the cups into a shaded area to cool. Wait 10 minutes. Record the temperature in each cup.

WHAT DO YOU THINK?

1. Which heats up faster—soil or water?

_____

2. Which cools faster?

_____

3. How might the heating and cooling rates of inland areas compare with those of coastal areas?

_____

_____

_____

_____

CHALLENGE

Will adding gravel to the soil change your results? Repeat the activity to test your prediction.

SECTION | DATASHEET
18.3 | Investigate Climate Change

How does blocking sunlight affect temperature?

MATERIALS white tissue paper, tape, 2 thermometers

PROCEDURE

1 Tape the tissue paper to the window frame to cover one window. If you cannot cover the whole window, adjust the blinds or shade so that sunlight enters that window only through the tissue paper. Leave a second window on the same side of the room uncovered.

2 Adjust the shade or blinds of the uncovered window so that sunlight enters the room through equal areas on both windows. Place a thermometer in front of each window. Record the temperature for each window.

3 Wait 15 minutes. Record the temperature for each window.

WHAT DO YOU THINK?

1. How did blocking one window with the tissue paper affect the temperature?

_____

2. What do you think caused this result?

_____

_____

CHALLENGE

How would adding a second layer of tissue paper to the covered window affect the results? Add the second layer and repeat the activity to test your prediction.

_____

_____

CHAPTER
18 | CHAPTER INVESTIGATION
Microclimates

OVERVIEW AND PURPOSE

Microclimates are local variations within a region's climate. Natural and artificial features such as beaches, hills, wooded areas, buildings, and pavement can cause such variations. Even trees planted around a house or parking lot may influence the climate of that small area. In this lab, you will use what you have learned about weather and climate to

- measure weather factors, such as air temperature, in two different microclimates
- discover how natural and artificial features affect local climate

<table>
<tr><td>MATERIALS</td></tr>
<tr><td>• 2 thermometers
• 2 other weather instruments of the same kind</td></tr>
</table>

Problem

How do natural and artificial features affect the climate of a small area?

Hypothesize

Write a hypothesis to explain how you expect the microclimates of two nearby locations to be affected by the different natural and artificial features in those areas. Your hypothesis should take the form of an "If … , then … , because …" statement. You should complete steps 1–3 in the procedure before writing your hypothesis.

_____

_____

Procedure

1 Work in a group of four students. You will use a thermometer to record air temperature. Choose another weather instrument that you have made or that is available to you. You might use a psychrometer to measure relative humidity, a barometer to measure air pressure, or an anemometer to measure wind speed.

2 Label the blank column to identify what you will measure with the instrument you chose in step 1.

Time (min.)	Location 1:		Location 2:	
	Temp (°C)		Temp (°C)	
0				
5				
10				

CHAPTER 18
Climate and Climate Change

③ Go outside the school with your teacher, taking your instruments, notebooks, and this lab book. Choose two locations near the school with different features for your group to study. For example, you might choose a grassy area and a paved area, or one area with trees and another area without trees.

④ Divide your group into two pairs. Each pair of students should have one thermometer and the other instrument you have chosen. You and your partner will study one location. The other pair will study the second location.

⑤ Decide ahead of time how you will control the variables. For example, both pairs might take measurements at a set height above the ground.

⑥ Draw pictures of the location you are studying in the box below. Write a description of the natural and artificial features in this area.

⑦ Set up the instruments in your location. Record the air temperature. Take follow-up readings five and ten minutes later. Take a reading with the other weather instrument each time you take a temperature reading.

⑧ Record data gathered by the other two members of your group in your data table. Calculate the average temperature for each location. Then calculate the average reading for the other weather factor that you measured. To find the averages add up each set of readings to get a sum. Then divide the sum by the number of readings.

Observe and Analyze

1. **Identify Variables and Constants** Identify the variables and constants in the investigation. List these factors in the table below.

Variables	Constants

2. **Compare and Contrast** Which average measurements in the two locations were the same? What differences did your investigations reveal? For example, was one area cooler or less windy than the other?

_____

_____

_____

CHAPTER 18
Climate and Climate Change

Conclude

1. Infer Answer the question posed in the problem.

_____

_____

_____

2. Interpret Compare your results with your hypothesis. Did the results support your hypothesis? Did the natural and artificial features have the effects you expected?

_____

_____

_____

_____

3. Evaluate What were the limitations of your instruments? What other sources of error could have affected the results?

_____

_____

_____

_____

4. Apply How could you apply the results of your investigation to help you make landscaping or building decisions? For example, what could you do to make a picnic area more comfortable?

_____

_____

_____

CHAPTER
18 ADDITIONAL INVESTIGATION
Modeling El Niño

OVERVIEW AND PURPOSE

You have learned that El Niño is a disturbance of wind patterns and ocean currents in the Pacific Ocean. You also know that El Niño occurs every 3 to 7 years and can last from one to one and a half years. In this investigation you will use what you have learned about El Niño to

- model the winds that cause this disturbance
- demonstrate how ocean currents change during El Niño

Problem

How does El Niño disturb Earth's wind patterns and ocean currents?

Hypothesize

El Niño is a short-term change in global weather patterns. Use what you know about global wind and water circulation patterns to form a hypothesis to explain what causes El Niño. Write your hypothesis as an "If . . ., then . . ., because" statement.

MATERIALS
- mineral oil (200 mL)
- plastic bowl
- two spoons
- red oil-based paint
- clear rectangular container
- water
- blue food coloring
- portable hair dryer

TIME
45 minutes

_____

_____

_____

_____

Procedure

1 Pour the mineral oil into the plastic bowl. Use one of the spoons to mix a spoonful of the red paint into the oil. Stir the oil until the paint is evenly distributed.

2 Slowly pour water into the container until it reaches 3 cm from the top.

3 Add 10 drops of blue food coloring to the water. Use the other, clean spoon to slowly mix the food coloring until it is evenly mixed into the water.

4 Slowly add the red mineral oil to the blue water.

5 Wait for the oil and water to separate.

6 Hold the hair dryer at an angle over the container, as shown in the diagram.

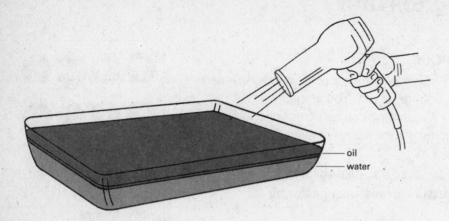

— oil
— water

7 Turn the hair dryer on medium and allow it to blow over the surface of the water for about 30 seconds. Observe what happens.

8 Turn the hair dryer off and observe what happens to the water and oil in the container.

9 Repeat steps 7 and 8 several times. Observe what happens each time you turn the hair dryer off. Record your observations in Table 1.

TABLE 1. MODELING EL NIÑO	
Trial	**Observation**
1	
2	
3	
4	
5	

CHAPTER 18
Climate and Climate Change

Observe and Analyze

1. **Explain** What do the red oil and the blue water in the model represent?

_____

_____

_____

2. **Model** Which global wind system does the air from the hair dryer represent?

_____

_____

3. **Describe** What happened to the oil and water as the air blew over it? Does this situation represent normal conditions or El Niño conditions?

_____

_____

_____

_____

4. **Describe** What happened when the air stopped blowing? Does this situation represent normal conditions or El Niño conditions?

_____

_____

_____

_____

_____

Conclude

1. **Explain** Explain what happens when strong trade winds blow from east to west over the Pacific Ocean. Think about air pressure, and think about the rain that falls.

_____

_____

_____

2. **Describe** When El Niño starts, what happens to the wind and the rains?

_____

_____

_____

3. **Describe** What is upwelling, and when during this investigation did you model this process?

_____

_____

_____

4. **Infer** Why is upwelling important?

_____

_____

_____

5. **Infer** Plants, animals, and many other organisms live in coastal waters. How do you think El Niño affects these organisms?

_____

_____

_____

SECTION
19.1 | DATASHEET
Constellation Wheel Sheet

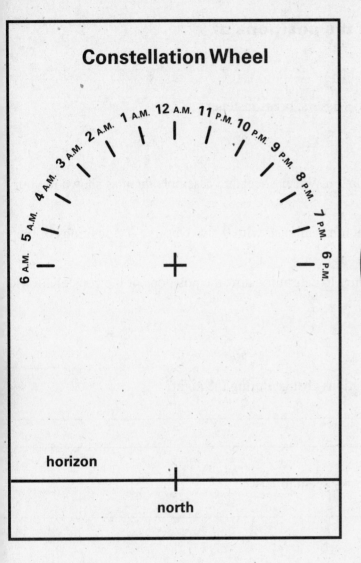

Constellation Wheel

horizon

north

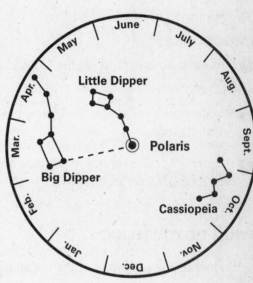

SECTION | DATASHEET
19.1 | Investigate Constellation Positions

How does time of day affect the positions of constellations?

MATERIALS Constellation Wheel Sheet, scissors, brass fastener

PROCEDURE

1 Cut out both diagrams on the Constellation Wheel Sheet and assemble them as shown in your textbook.

2 Rotate the wheel so that the current month is aligned with 9 P.M. Observe the positions of the constellations.

3 Align the current month with other times to determine how the positions of the constellations change during the night.

WHAT DO YOU THINK?

1. How do the positions of the constellations change during the night?

_____

_____

2. In which direction does the northern sky seem to turn?

_____

CHALLENGE

Earth's rotation makes the sky seem to turn. What does the model tell you about the direction of Earth's rotation?

_____

_____

SECTION
19.3
DATASHEET
Investigate Launch Planning

How does Earth's rotation affect launches of spacecraft?

MATERIALS paper, small bucket, large bucket

PROCEDURE

1 Tightly wad 14 sheets of paper into balls, and place the balls in a small bucket.

2 Stand 1.5 m away from a large bucket placed on a desk. Try tossing 7 balls into the bucket.

3 While turning slowly, try tossing the remaining 7 balls into the bucket.

WHAT DO YOU THINK?

1. How much more difficult was it to toss the paper balls into the bucket while you were turning than when you were standing still?

_____

_____

2. Why does Earth's rotation make launching rockets into space more complicated?

_____

_____

CHALLENGE

How would you design an experiment to show the variables involved in a launch from Earth toward another rotating body in space, such as the Moon?

_____

_____

_____

_____

_____

_____

CHAPTER 19
Exploring Space

SECTION
DATASHEET
19.4 | Investigate Weathering

How does weather affect evidence of impacts on Earth?

MATERIALS 2 shoebox lids, sand, ruler, golf ball, meter stick

PROCEDURE

1 Fill a shoebox lid halfway with sand, and smooth the surface with a ruler.

2 Create three craters by dropping a golf ball into the sand from a height of 70 cm. Remove the ball carefully. Leave the lid inside the classroom.

3 Repeat steps 1 and 2 outdoors, leaving the lid in an area where it will be exposed to the weather.

4 Check both lids after 24 hours. Observe changes in each one.

WHAT DO YOU THINK?

1. How did the craters in the sand that you left outdoors differ in appearance from the craters in the sand that remained inside?

   _____

   _____

2. What aspect of weather caused any differences you observed?

   _____

CHALLENGE

What natural processes besides weather can affect evidence of impacts from space objects on Earth?

_____

_____

CHAPTER 19
Exploring Space

CHAPTER
19 | CHAPTER INVESTIGATION
Observing Spectra

OVERVIEW AND PURPOSE

Visible light is made up of different colors that can be separated into a rainbow band called a spectrum. Astronomers gain information about the characteristics of stars by spreading their light into spectra (*spectra* is the plural form of *spectrum*). A spectroscope is a device that produces spectra. In most spectroscopes, diffraction gratings are used to separate light into different colors. The colors with the longest wavelengths appear farthest from the slit in a spectroscope. The colors with the shortest wavelengths appear closest to the slit. In this investigation you will

MATERIALS
- shoebox with lid
- ruler
- scissors
- diffraction grating
- tape
- index card
- pencils or markers in a variety of colors
- incandescent light
- fluorescent light

- build a spectroscope and observe the spectra of three different light sources
- identify ways in which the spectra of light sources differ

Procedure

1 Cut a hole measuring 3 cm × 1.5 cm in each end of a shoebox. Make sure that the holes line up.

2 On the inside of the box, tape a piece of diffraction grating over one of the holes. Handle the diffraction grating by its edges so that you do not get fingerprints on it.

3 Cut an index card in half, and tape the halves over the outside of the other hole as shown. Leave a very narrow slit between the two halves of the index card.

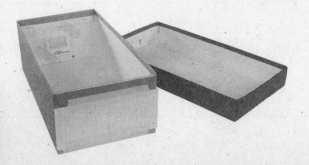

④ Put the lid on the box. Then turn off the overhead lights in the classroom.

⑤ Look through the hole covered with the diffraction grating, aiming the slit at the sky through a window. **Caution:** *Never look directly at the Sun.* Observe the spectrum you see to the left of the slit.

⑥ Repeat step 5 while aiming the spectroscope at an incandescent light and then at a fluorescent light.

Observe and Analyze

1. **Record Observations** For each light source, draw in Table 1 the spectrum you see to the left of the slit. Describe the colors and patterns in the spectrum, and label the light source.

TABLE 1. SPECTRA OF DIFFERENT LIGHT SOURCES		
Light Source	**Drawing**	**Description**

2. Identify Limits What problems, if any, did you experience in observing the spectra? Why was it important to turn off overhead lights for this activity?

_____

_____

Conclude

1. Compare and Contrast How did the spectra differ from one another? Did you notice any stripes of color that were brighter or narrower than other colors in the same spectrum? Did you notice any lines or spaces separating colors?

_____

_____

2. Analyze The shorter the wavelength of a color, the closer it appears to the slit in a spectroscope. On the basis of your observations, which color has the shortest wavelength? Which color has the longest wavelength?

_____

_____

3. Identify Limits How might the spectra look different if the slit at the end of the spectroscope were curved instead of a straight line?

_____

_____

CHAPTER 19
Exploring Space

CHAPTER | ADDITIONAL INVESTIGATION
19 | # A Simple Refracting Telescope

OVERVIEW AND PURPOSE

You've learned that telescopes can be used to study objects far from Earth. Also recall that there are two main types of telescopes. In a refracting telescope, one lens gathers light to form an image of the object being viewed. Another lens in a refracting telescope magnifies the image. In this investigation you will

- make a simple refracting telescope
- use the telescope to view distant objects

MATERIALS
- two mailing tubes (One must have a slightly smaller diameter than the other.)
- ruler or meter stick
- serrated knife
- corrugated cardboard
- drawing compass
- scissors
- 2 convex lenses with different focal lengths
- glue

TIME
45 minutes

Procedure

1. Use the focal lengths of your lenses to determine how long to make the body of the telescope. Add the focal lengths. Record this number on the first line below. Now divide this number by 2. Record this value on the second line. Add 3 cm to this number and record this value on the third line below. This last number will be the length of each tube of your telescope.

    total of focal lengths _____ cm

    total of focal lengths divided by 2 _____ cm

    total of focal lengths divided by 2 plus 3 cm _____ cm

2. Use the meter stick and a pencil to mark each mailing tube with the length you recorded on the third line above.

3. Carefully use the serrated knife to cut each mailing tube to the correct length.

4. Use the ruler to measure the diameter of the inside of each mailing tube. Write these values below.

    diameter of inside of smaller tube _____ cm

    diameter of inside of larger tube _____ cm

5. Use the compass to make a circle with the diameter equal to that of the inside of the smaller tube on the corrugated cardboard.

6 Use the compass to make a circle with the diameter equal to that of the lens with the shorter focal length on the cardboard. Your drawing should look like the one shown below.

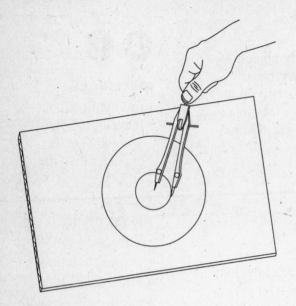

7 Use the scissors to cut around the outer diameter. Then carefully cut out the inner circle, as shown below.

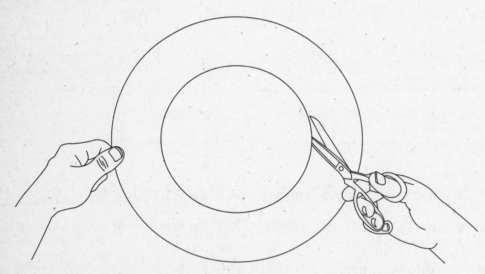

8 Glue the lens with the shorter focal length into the circle. Be careful not to get glue on the surface of the lens. Allow the glue to dry completely.

9 Use the compass to make a circle with the diameter equal to that of the inside of the larger tube on the corrugated cardboard.

10 Use the compass to make a circle with the diameter equal to that of the lens with the longer focal length on the cardboard.

11 Use the scissors to cut around the outer diameter. Then carefully cut out the inner circle, as you did before.

12 Glue the lens with the longer focal length into this new circle. Be careful not to get glue on the surface of the lens. Allow the glue to dry completely.

13 Assemble your telescope as shown below. Slide the tube with the smaller diameter into the tube with the larger diameter. Then glue the lens holders into place. Allow the glue to dry completely.

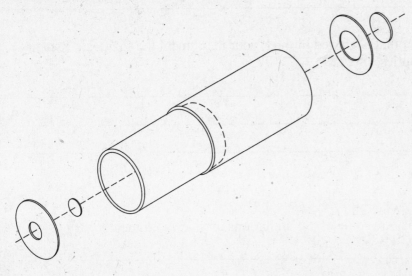

14 Use your telescope to view distant objects. *CAUTION: Do not use your telescope or any telescope to view the Sun directly. Doing so could cause permanent damage to your eyes.*

Observe and Analyze

1. Explain Which of your lenses is the eyepiece lens? What is the function of the eyepiece lens?

_____

_____

_____

2. Explain Which of your lenses is the objective lens? What is the function of the objective lens?

_____

_____

_____

3. Describe Are the images viewed through your instrument upright or inverted?

_____

_____

_____

CHAPTER 19
Exploring Space

4. Describe What happens to the images viewed as you slide the inner tube into and out of the larger tube?

_____

_____

_____

5. Explain When is an object that is viewed through your instrument the sharpest? Explain your answer in terms of optics.

_____

_____

_____

Conclude

1. Identify Limitations What are some of the limitations of your instrument?

_____

_____

_____

2. Infer Name two ways in which you could improve your instrument.

_____

_____

_____

3. Predict What would happen if you were to reconstruct your instrument using a larger objective lens?

_____

_____

_____

4. Apply You made a simple refracting telescope. Most astronomical telescopes are reflecting telescopes. Why?

_____

_____

_____

DATASHEET
Explore Time Zones

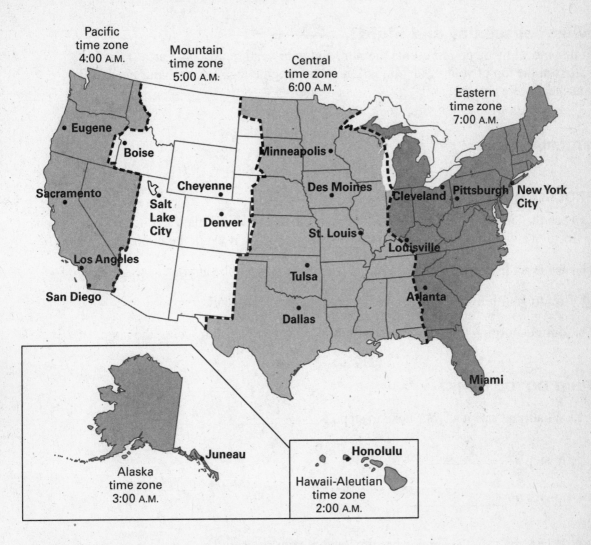

Pacific
time zone
4:00 A.M.

Mountain
time zone
5:00 A.M.

Central
time zone
6:00 A.M.

Eastern
time zone
7:00 A.M.

Eugene

Boise

Sacramento

Cheyenne

Salt
Lake
City

Denver

Minneapolis

Des Moines

Cleveland   Pittsburgh   New York
City

St. Louis

Los Angeles

Louisville

San Diego

Tulsa

Atlanta

Dallas

Miami

Juneau

Alaska
time zone
3:00 A.M.

Honolulu

Hawaii-Aleutian
time zone
2:00 A.M.

The label for each time zone gives the zone's time at noon GMT.
Iceland is in the same time zone as the prime meridian, thus it is noon
in Iceland at noon GMT.

20.1 Investigate Rotation

What causes day and night?

In this model the lamp represents the Sun, and your head represents Earth. The North Pole is at the top of your head. You will need to imagine locations on your head as if your head were a globe.

MATERIALS lamp

PROCEDURE

1 Face the lamp and hold your hands to your face. Your hands mark the horizon. For a person located at your nose, the Sun would be high in the sky. It would be noon.

2 Face away from the lamp. Determine what time it would be at your nose.

3 Turn to your left until you see the lamp along your left hand.

4 Continue turning to the left, through noon, until you just stop seeing the lamp.

WHAT DO YOU THINK?

1. What time was it at your nose in step 2? _____

   in step 3? _____

   in step 4? _____

2. When you face the lamp, what time is it at your right ear?

   _____

CHALLENGE

How can a cloud be bright even when it is dark on the ground?

_____

_____

_____

SECTION DATASHEET
20.2 Investigate Moon Features

How did the Moon's features form?

In this model, you will use a paper napkin to represent the Moon's surface and gelatin to represent molten rock from inside the Moon.

MATERIALS liquid gelatin, clear plastic cup, paper towel, bowl of ice

PROCEDURE

1 Pour about 1 cm of partly cooled liquid gelatin into the cup.

2 Hold the paper towel by bringing its corners together. Push the towel into the cup until the center of the towel touches the bottom of the cup. Open the towel slightly.

3 Place the cup in the bowl of ice, and allow the gelatin time to solidify.

WHAT DO YOU THINK?

1. What part of the towel did the gelatin affect?

_____

2. When you look down into the cup, what can the smooth areas tell you about heights?

_____

_____

CHALLENGE

Early astronomers thought there might be oceans on the Moon. How does your model lava resemble an ocean?

_____

_____

_____

CHAPTER 20
Earth, Moon, and Sun

SECTION | DATASHEET
20.3 | Investigate Phases of the Moon

Why does the Moon seem to change shape?

MATERIALS foam ball, stick, lamp

PROCEDURE

1. Place the ball on the stick, which will act as a handle. The ball will represent the Moon, and your head will represent Earth.

2. Hold the ball toward the light, then move it to your left until you see a bright edge. Draw what you see on a separate sheet of paper.

3. Move the ball farther around until half of what you see is lit. Draw it.

4. Keep moving the ball around to your left until the side you see is fully lit, then half lit, then lit only a little bit. Each time, face the ball and draw it.

WHAT DO YOU THINK?

1. In step 2, which side of the ball was lit? Explain why.

   _____

   _____

2. How are your drawings like the photographs of the Moon's phases? Label each drawing above with the name of the corresponding lunar phase.

   _____

   _____

CHALLENGE

When the Moon is a crescent, sometimes you can dimly see the rest of the Moon if you look closely. Where might the light that makes the darker part of the Moon visible come from?

_____

CHAPTER 20
Earth, Moon, and Sun

CHAPTER
20 | **CHAPTER INVESTIGATION**
Modeling Seasons

OVERVIEW AND PURPOSE

Why is the weather in North America so much colder in January than in July? You might be surprised to learn that it has nothing to do with Earth's distance from the Sun. In fact, Earth is closest to the Sun in January. In this investigation, you will model the cause of seasons as you

- orient a light source at different angles to a surface
- determine how the angles of sunlight at a location change as Earth orbits the Sun

MATERIALS
- graph paper
- flashlight
- meter stick
- protractor
- globe
- stack of books
- sticky note

Problem

How does the angle of light affect the amount of solar energy a location receives at different times of year?

Hypothesize

After you complete step 4, write a hypothesis to explain how the angles of sunlight affect the amounts of solar energy your location receives at different times of year. Your hypothesis should take the form of an "If . . . , then . . . , because . . ." statement.

_____

_____

Procedure

PART A

1. Mark an X near the center of the graph paper. Shine the flashlight onto the paper from about 30 cm straight above the X—at an angle of 90° to the surface. Observe the size of the spot of light.

2 Shine the flashlight onto the X at different angles. Keep the flashlight at the same distance. Write down what happens to the size of the spot of light as you change angles.

_____

_____

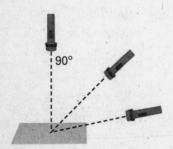

3 Repeat step 2, but observe just one square near the X. Write down what happens to the brightness of the light as you change the angle. The brightness shows how much energy the area receives from the flashlight.

_____

_____

4 Think about the temperatures at different times of year at your location, then write your hypothesis.

PART B

5 Set up the globe, books, and flashlight as shown in the photograph. Point the globe's North Pole to the right. This position represents solstice A.

6 Find your location on the globe. Place a folded sticky note onto the globe at your location as shown in the photograph. Rotate the globe on its axis until the note faces toward the flashlight.

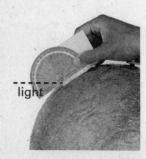

TABLE 1. SOLSTICES A AND B		
	Solstice A	**Solstice B**
Drawing		
Angle of light (°)		
Observations		

7 The flashlight beam represents noonday sunlight at your location. Use the protractor to estimate the angle of the light on the surface.

8 Move the globe to the left side of the table and the flashlight and books to the right side of the table. Point the North Pole to the right. This position represents solstice B.

9 Repeat step 7 for solstice B.

Observe and Analyze

1. **Record** In Table 1, draw the setup of your materials in each part of the investigation. Organize your notes.

2. **Analyze** Describe how the angle of the flashlight in step 2 affected the area of the spot of light. Which angle concentrated the light into the smallest area?

_____

_____

3. **Evaluate** At which angle did a square of the graph paper receive the most energy?

_____

_____

4. **Compare** Compare the angles of light in steps 7 and 9. In which position was the angle of light closer to 90°?

_____

_____

Conclude

1. **Evaluate** How did the angle of sunlight at your location differ at the two times of year? At which position is sunlight more concentrated at your location?

_____

_____

2. **Apply** The amount of solar energy at a location affects temperature. Which solstice—A or B—represents the summer solstice at your location?

_____

_____

3. **Interpret** Do your results support your hypothesis? Explain why or why not.

_____

_____

CHAPTER | ADDITIONAL INVESTIGATION

20 | Making an Equatorial Sundial

OVERVIEW AND PURPOSE

Throughout history, people have used the position of the Sun and resulting shadows to tell time. In this activity, you will

- make and set up a simple sundial
- use the sundial to estimate the time of day

MATERIALS
- dial template
- scissors
- glue
- latitude ruler
- thin stick

TIME
45 minutes

Procedure

1 Cut out the stiff dial template and fold it carefully along the dashed line. Make sure the dial faces are lined up, then glue the halves in place.

2 Poke a small hole in the center of the circle.

3 Find out your latitude from an atlas, the Internet, or your teacher. Put a mark on the latitude ruler for your latitude. You may need to estimate it.

4 Mark one end of the stick to be the bottom. Place this end of the stick at the line marked "bottom" on the latitude ruler. Measure the stick to your latitude line and mark this distance on the stick.

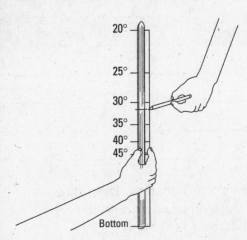

5 Push the top of the stick into the center of the south face of the dial. Adjust the stick so the dial is at the latitude mark. Make sure the dial is perpendicular to the stick.

CHAPTER 20
Earth, Moon, and Sun

6 On a sunny day, take the sundial outside. Carefully point the top end of the stick north. Rest the bottom of the stick and the folded bottom of the dial on a flat surface as in the diagram.

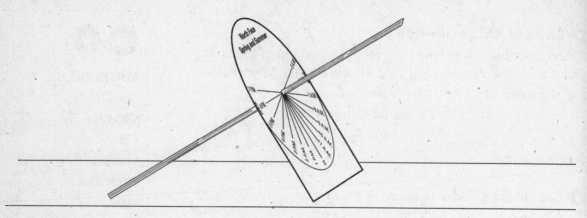

7 The shadow of the stick will fall on either the sundial's north face or its south face. Use the center of the shadow to estimate the time several times during the day.

Observe and Analyze

1. Record For each measurement, write down the clock time, the sundial time, and which of the two dial faces you needed to use. Record your answers in Table 1.

TABLE 1. SUNDIAL DATA				
Clock time				
Sundial time				
Sundial face used				
Difference (min.)				

2. Calculate Compare the sundial time to the time from a watch or clock. Determine whether the sundial's reading is ahead or behind the clock time and by how much. Use the space below for your calculations. Record the differences in Table 1.

3. **Evaluate** If the sundial is set up well, the sundial's reading will be ahead or behind the clock time by the same amount of time for all your observations. How well was your sundial set up?

_____

_____

Conclude

1. **Identify Limits** How would you change what you did now that you have seen some results?

_____

_____

_____

_____

2. **Evaluate** Would your sundial be good to use to help you get to school on time? Would your sundial be good to use on a picnic to help you decide when to eat lunch?

_____

_____

_____

3. **Apply** Many sundials are set up to stay in place for years at a time. Why might this be useful?

_____

_____

_____

CHAPTER 20
Earth, Moon, and Sun

Latitude Ruler

20° —
25° —
30° —
35° —
40° —
45° —
50° —
55° —
60° —

Bottom —

Dial Template

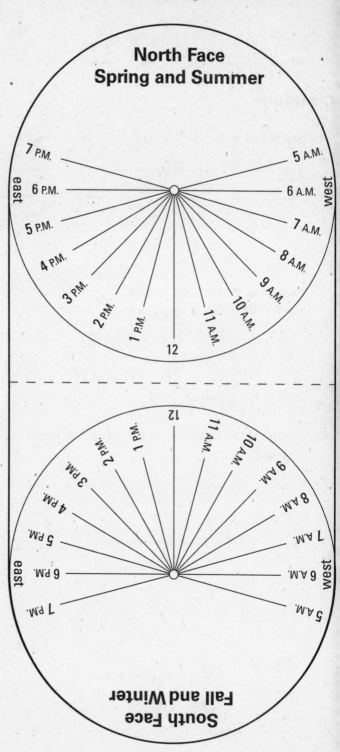

North Face
Spring and Summer

7 P.M.   5 A.M.
east   6 P.M.   6 A.M.   west
5 P.M.   7 A.M.
4 P.M.   8 A.M.
3 P.M.   9 A.M.
2 P.M.   10 A.M.
1 P.M.   11 A.M.
12

12
2 P.M.   1 P.M.   11 A.M.
3 P.M.   10 A.M.
4 P.M.   9 A.M.
5 P.M.   8 A.M.
east   6 P.M.   7 A.M.   west
7 P.M.   6 A.M.
5 A.M.

South Face
Fall and Winter

Name _____ Period _____ Date _____

SECTION 21.1 | DATASHEET
Planetary Distance Table

CHAPTER 21 Our Solar System

Object	Position (sheets from Sun)
Sun	0.0
Mercury	1.9
Venus	3.6
Earth	5.0
Mars	7.6
Jupiter	26.0
Saturn	47.8
Uranus	96.1
Neptune	150.6
Pluto	197.7

SPACE SCIENCE, CHAPTER 21, DATASHEET 241

SECTION | DATASHEET
21.1 | Investigate Distances

How far apart are the planets?

MATERIALS roll of toilet paper, felt-tipped pen, Distance Table

PROCEDURE

1 Mark one sheet from the end of the roll of paper as the location of the Sun. Mark an X and write the word Sun with dots rather than lines.

2 Use the Distance Table data sheet to mark the distances for the rest of the solar system. Count sheets and estimate tenths of a sheet as necessary. Re-roll or fold the paper neatly.

3 Go to a space where you can unroll the paper. Compare the distances of planets as you walk along the paper and back again.

WHAT DO YOU THINK?

1. How does the distance between Earth and Mars compare with the distance between Saturn and Uranus?

_____

_____

_____

2. How would you use the spacing to sort the planets into groups?

_____

_____

_____

CHALLENGE

If it took two years for the Voyager 2 spacecraft to travel from Earth to Jupiter, about how long do you think it took for Voyager 2 to travel from Jupiter to Neptune?

_____

_____

SECTION
DATASHEET
21.2 Investigate Layers

How do the layers inside of planets form?

MATERIALS container, spoon, firm gelatin, sand, wax pieces, bowl of hot tap water

PROCEDURE

1 Put pieces of gelatin into the container until it is about one-quarter full.

2 Mix in a spoonful each of sand and wax. Use the spoon to break the gelatin into small pieces as you mix. Remove the spoon.

3 Place the container in a bowl of hot tap water (about 70°C) and observe what happens as the gelatin melts.

WHAT DO YOU THINK?

1. What happened to each of the materials when the gelatin melted?

_____

_____

2. How do the results resemble the core, mantle, and crust of Earth and other planets?

_____

_____

_____

_____

CHALLENGE

How might you improve this model?

_____

_____

_____

SECTION | DATASHEET
21.3 | Investigate Giant Planets

Why do Saturn's rings seem to change size?

MATERIALS ice-cream stick, disposable plate, scissors, clay

PROCEDURE

1 Poke the stick through the plate and cut off the plate's rim. Shape the clay onto both sides of the plate to make a model of a planet with rings.

2 Model Saturn's orbit for your partner. Stand between your partner and the classroom clock. Point one end of the stick at the clock. Hold the model at the same height as your partner's eyes. Have your partner watch the model with just one eye open.

3 Move one step counterclockwise around your partner and point the stick at the clock again. Make sure the model is as high as your partner's eyes. Your partner may need to turn to see the model.

4 Continue taking steps around your partner and pointing the stick at the clock until you have moved the model all the way around your partner.

5 Switch roles with your partner and repeat steps 2, 3, and 4.

WHAT DO YOU THINK?

1. How did your view of the rings change as the model planet changed position?

_____

_____

2. How many times per orbit do the rings seem to vanish?

_____

CHALLENGE

How do Saturn's axis and orbit compare with those of Earth?

_____

_____

CHAPTER | CHAPTER INVESTIGATION
21 | **Exploring Impact Craters**

OVERVIEW AND PURPOSE

Nearly 50,000 years ago, an asteroid plummeted through
Earth's atmosphere and exploded near what is now Winslow,
Arizona. The resulting impact crater is about 1.2 km (0.7 mi)
wide. Most of the other craters on Earth have been erased.
However, some planets and most moons in the solar system
have surfaces that are covered with craters. In this investigation
you will

- use solid objects to make craters in a flour surface
- determine how one variable affects the resulting crater

MATERIALS
- newspapers
- container
- flour
- colored powder
- several objects
- meter stick
- ruler
- balance

Problem

How does one characteristic of an impact or a colliding object
affect the resulting crater?

Hypothesize

Complete steps 1–5 before writing your problem statement and hypothesis.

_____

_____

Procedure

1 Place the container on newspapers, and add flour to a depth of 2–4 cm. Stir the
flour to break up any lumps, and then smooth the surface with a ruler. Sprinkle
the top with colored powder.

2 Drop an object into the flour from waist height, then carefully remove it without
disturbing the flour. Use the diagram to identify the various parts of the impact
crater you made.

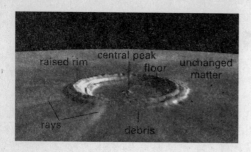

3 To help you design your experiment, try several cratering methods. Make each new crater in a different location in the container. If your container becomes too full of craters, stir the flour, smooth it, and sprinkle on more colored powder.

4 Design an experiment to test the effects of a variable. Choose just one variable to change—the height, the size or mass of the object, or perhaps the fluffiness of the flour. Determine how much you need to change your variable in order to get results different enough to see.

_____

_____

5 Experiment to find some part of the crater that is affected by changing your variable, such as the depth, the size of the blanket of debris, or the number of rays. Design your experiment so that you measure the part of the crater that changes the most.

_____

6 Now that you have identified a variable to test, write a specific problem statement by completing the question.

How does _____

affect _____?

Write a hypothesis to explain how changing this variable will affect the crater. Your hypothesis should take the form of an "If . . . , then . . . , because . . ." statement.

_____

_____

7 Perform your experiment. Do not change any factors except your chosen variable.

8 Make several trials for each value of your variable, because there are some factors you cannot control.

9 Record measurements and other observations, and make drawings as you go along.

Observe and Analyze

1. Record Use a diagram to show how you measure the craters.

Record your measurements in Table 1.

TABLE 1. DATA AND AVERAGES					
Variable:	Result:				
	Trial 1	Trial 2	Trial 3	Average	Notes

2. Identify Variables List the variables and constants. The independent variable is the factor that you changed. The dependent variable is affected by this change. Use these definitions when you graph your results.

_____

_____

3. **Calculate** Determine averages by adding all of your measurements at each value of your independent variable, then dividing the sum by the number of measurements. Record the results in Table 1.

4. **Graph** Make a line graph of your average results on a sheet of graph paper. Place the independent variable on the horizontal axis and the dependent variable on the vertical axis. Why should you use a line graph instead of a bar graph for these data?

_____

_____

Conclude

1. **Analyze** Answer your problem statement. Do your data support your hypothesis?

_____

_____

2. **Evaluate** Did you identify a trend in your results? Is your experiment a failure if you did not identify a trend? Why or why not?

_____

_____

_____

3. **Identify Limits** How would you modify the design of your experiment now that you have seen the results?

_____

_____

_____

4. **Apply** What do you think would happen if a colliding object hit water instead of land?

_____

_____

CHAPTER 21 | ADDITIONAL INVESTIGATION
Exploring Ellipses

OVERVIEW AND PURPOSE

You have learned that Earth, like its solar system neighbors, orbits the Sun in a closed, elongated curve called an ellipse. The Sun is located at one of the foci of the ellipse. In this investigation, you will

- construct several ellipses
- calculate the eccentricity, or flatness, of each ellipse you drew
- calculate the eccentricities of the orbits made by the planets in our solar system
- compare and contrast the eccentricities of the planets in our solar system

MATERIALS
- plain white paper
- pinboard
- metric ruler
- 3 small upholstery tacks each about 2 cm long
- 3 sharp, different colored pencils
- string
- scissors
- calculator

TIME
45 minutes

Problem

Read through the Materials list and the Procedure for this investigation. How will you use the materials to construct ellipses? If you move the tacks farther apart and draw a new shape, how do you think the two shapes will compare?

Hypothesis

Write a hypothesis to describe how the eccentricity of a planet's orbit would depend on the orbit's shape. Your hypothesis should take the form of an "If . . . , then . . . , because . . ." statement.

_____

_____

_____

Procedure

PART A

❶ Fold the paper in half lengthwise, then fold it in half crosswise to make quarters. Open the paper and put it on the pinboard. You will make measurements along the long fold of the paper.

❷ Measure from the center of the paper 8 cm to the right. Mark the point and circle it. This is where you will place the tying tack for each ellipse.

❸ Use the ruler and the first colored pencil to measure and mark points 2 cm to the left and 2 cm to the right of the center point, along the fold. Each point will be a focus (plural: foci) for the first ellipse.

4 Place tacks at all three of your marks, as shown. About 1/2 cm of each tack should be visible above the paper.

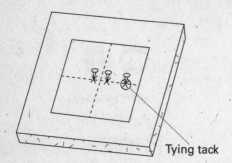

Tying tack

5 Cut a length of string about 40 cm long. While your partner holds the tacks in place, tie the string in a snug loop around the three tacks. Remove the tying tack. Gently tug on the string to make sure the knot is secure. If the string comes untied, replace the tying tack and tie the string again.

6 Make sure the string is looped around the tacks. Ask your partner to hold the tacks in place as you put the colored pencil into the loop and pull the string taut.

7 While your partner holds the tacks in place, move the pencil in a circular motion to produce an ellipse, as shown below. You may need to draw half the figure at a time. Remember to keep the string taut as your construct the figure.

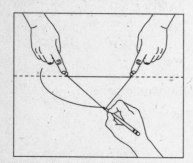

8 Use the metric ruler to measure the length of the major axis, L, and the distance between the foci, d, on your ellipse, using the figure below as a guide. Record these measurements in Table 1 next to the color of this ellipse.

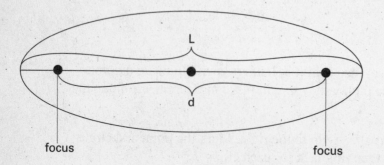

focus   focus

9 Construct two more ellipses. Repeat steps 3–8, but increase the distance of the foci a few centimeters for each new ellipse and use a different colored pencil.

10 Calculate the eccentricity, or flatness, of each ellipse you drew using the following formula: e = d/L. You should get a number between zero and one. Record the eccentricities in Table 1.

TABLE 1. MEASUREMENTS AND ECCENTRICITIES OF DIFFERENT ELLIPSES

Ellipse	Color	Distance between tacks and center (cm)	Major axis, L (cm)	Distance between foci, d (cm)	Eccentricity of the ellipse, e
1		2			
2					
3					

PART B

11 Use a calculator and the data in Table 2 to compute the eccentricity of the orbit of each planet in our solar system. Record your results in the appropriate places in the table.

TABLE 2. ECCENTRICITIES OF THE PATHS OF OUR SOLAR SYSTEM PLANETS

Planet	Mercury	Venus	Earth	Mars	Jupiter	Saturn	Uranus	Neptune	Pluto
Length of major axis, L (AU)*	0.774	1.446	2.000	3.048	10.406	19.080	38.360	60.120	78.880
Distance between foci, d (AU)*	0.016	0.010	0.034	0.284	0.500	1.068	1.802	0.542	19.642
Eccentricity, e (d/L)									

*An AU is an astronomical unit, which is equal to the average distance between Earth and the Sun. This distance is about 149.6×10^6 km.

Observe and Analyze

1. Describe Describe the shape of each ellipse by comparing it to a circle.

_____

_____

_____

2. Observe What happened to the shape of the ellipse when you increased the distance between the tacks?

_____

_____

_____

3. Observe Compare the eccentricity of each planet's orbit to the eccentricity of the ellipses you drew. Are any similar to an ellipse you drew? If so, which planet(s) and which ellipse(s)?

_____

_____

_____

4. Infer Would you move the pins closer together or farther apart to draw the shape of Earth's orbit?

_____

_____

_____

_____

Conclude

1. Identify Use the data in Table 2 to identify the planet with the most eccentric orbit. Identify the planet with the least eccentric orbit.

_____

_____

_____

2. Apply Which two planetary orbits are most circular?

_____

_____

_____

How does the distance of an object affect parallax?

MATERIALS meter stick, capped pen

PROCEDURE

1 Stand 1 m away from a classmate. Have the classmate hold up a meter stick at eye level.

2 With your left eye closed, hold a capped pen up close to your face. Look at the pen with your right eye, and line it up with the zero mark on the meter stick. Then open your left eye and quickly close your right eye. Observe how many centimeters the pen seems to move. Record your observation.

_____
_____

3 Repeat step 2 with the pen held at arm's length and then with the pen held at half your arm's length. Record your observation each time.

_____
_____
_____
_____

WHAT DO YOU THINK?

1. How many centimeters did the pen appear to move each time you observed it?

_____
_____

2. How is parallax affected when you change the distance of the pen from you?

_____
_____

CHALLENGE

How could you use this method to estimate distances that you cannot measure directly?

_____
_____

CHAPTER 22
Stars, Galaxies, and the Universe

DATASHEET
Galaxy Photo Sheet

CHAPTER 22
Stars, Galaxies, and the Universe

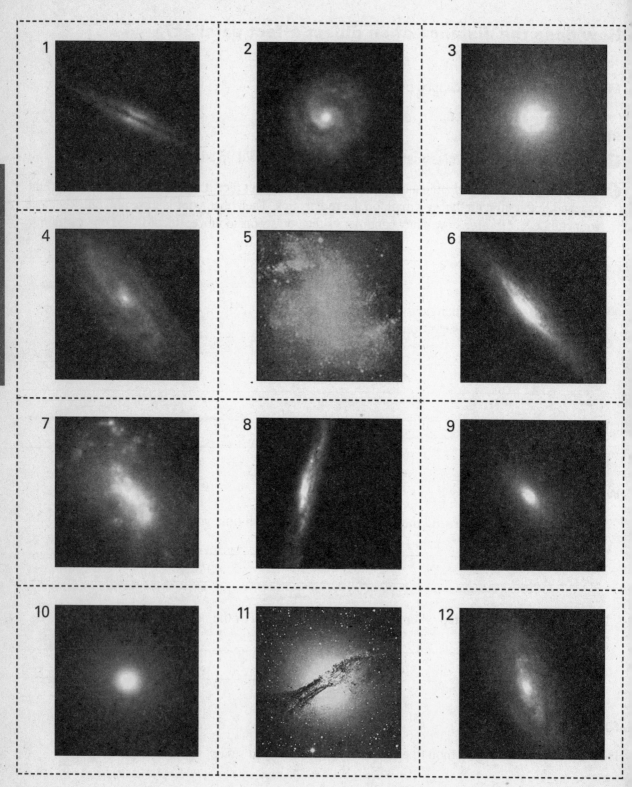

SECTION **22.3** | DATASHEET
Investigate Galaxy Shapes

How can you classify galaxies according to shape?

MATERIALS: Galaxy Photo Sheet, scissors

PROCEDURE

1 Cut out the photographs of galaxies on the Galaxy Photo Sheet.

2 Sort the galaxies into different groups according to their shapes. You may need a group for galaxies that do not fit in other groups.

WHAT DO YOU THINK?

1. How many groups did you sort the galaxies into?

_____

2. Describe each group briefly, and list which galaxies you put in each group.

_____

_____

_____

_____

CHALLENGE

What is the connection between the apparent shape of a galaxy and the galaxy's relationship to the viewer? **Hint:** Think about how an edge-on view of a compact disc differs from a view of it lying flat on a table.

_____

_____

_____

SECTION | DATASHEET
22.4 | Investigate Galaxies

How does the universe expand?

MATERIALS thick rubber band cut open, ballpoint pen, ruler

PROCEDURE

1 Spread the cut rubber band against the ruler without stretching it. Mark off every centimeter for 6 centimeters.

2 Align the first mark on the rubber band with the 1-centimeter mark on the ruler and hold it in place tightly. Stretch the rubber band so that the second mark is next to the 3-centimeter mark on the ruler.

3 Observe how many centimeters each mark has moved from its original location against the ruler.

WHAT DO YOU THINK?

1. How far did each mark on the rubber band move from its original location?

   _____

2. What does this activity demonstrate about the expansion of the universe?

   _____

   _____

   _____

CHALLENGE

How could you calculate the rates at which the marks moved when you stretched the rubber band?

   _____

   _____

   _____

CHAPTER | DATASHEET
22 | Photometer Assembly

Procedure for assembling the wax photometer

1 Cut out a 12 cm x 12 cm piece of aluminum foil

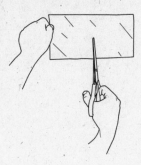

2 Fold the foil so that the shiny side faces out on both sides.

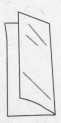

3 Place the aluminum foil between two paraffin blocks so that the blocks cover the foil.

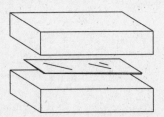

4 Wrap two rubber bands around the blocks near the edges to hold the photometer together.

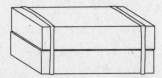

CHAPTER 22
Stars, Galaxies, and the Universe

CHAPTER INVESTIGATION
22 | Temperature, Brightness, and Color

OVERVIEW AND PURPOSE

Think of the metal heating surface on a hot plate. How can you tell whether the hot plate is fully heated? Is the metal surface brighter or dimmer than when it is just starting to get warm? Does the color of the surface change as the hot plate gets hotter? You may already have an idea of how temperature, brightness, and color are related—at least when it comes to heated metal. Do the same relationships apply to electric lights? to stars? This investigation is designed to help you find out. You will

- construct a wax photometer to compare the brightnesses and colors of different light sources
- determine how the temperature of a light source affects its brightness and color

MATERIALS
- 2 paraffin blocks
- aluminum foil
- 2 rubber bands
- 2 light-bulb holders
- 2 miniature light bulbs
- 3 AA batteries
- 4 pieces of uninsulated copper wire 15 cm long

Problem

How are brightness and color related to temperature?

Hypothesize

Write a hypothesis to explain how brightness and color are related to temperature. Your hypothesis should take the form of an "If . . . , then . . . , because . . ." statement.

_____

_____

Procedure

❶ An instrument called a photometer makes it easier to compare the brightnesses and colors of different light sources. Assemble the wax photometer as shown in the Photometer Assembly datasheet. The aluminum foil between the wax blocks should be folded so that the shiny side faces out on both sides.

2 Hold the photometer so that you can see both blocks. Bring it to different locations in the classroom, and observe how the brightnesses and colors of the blocks change as the two sides of the photometer are exposed to different light conditions.

3 Tape a piece of copper wire to each end of a battery, and connect the wires to a light-bulb holder. The battery will provide electricity to heat up the wire inside a light bulb.

4 Tape the negative terminal, or flat end, of one battery to the positive terminal of another battery. Tape a piece of copper wire to each end, and connect the wires to a light-bulb holder. Because two batteries will provide electricity to the bulb in this holder, the wire in the bulb will be hotter than the wire in the bulb powered by one battery.

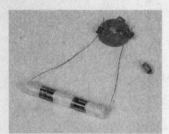

5 With the room darkened, insert a bulb into each light-bulb holder. If the bulb connected to two batteries does not light up, you may need to press the two batteries together with your fingers.

6 Place the photometer halfway between the two light bulbs. Compare the brightnesses of the two light sources. Record your observations in Table 1.

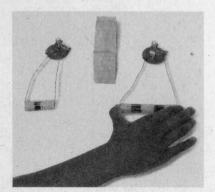

TABLE 1. PROPERTIES OF LIGHT FROM TWO SOURCES		
	Cooler Bulb (one battery)	**Warmer Bulb (two batteries)**
Brightness		
Color		

7 Move the photometer closer to the cooler bulb until both sides of the photometer are equally bright. Compare the colors of the two light sources. Record your observations in Table 1. To avoid draining the batteries, remove the bulbs from the holders when you have completed this step.

Observe and Analyze

1. **Record Observations** Draw the setup of your photometer and light sources. Be sure your data table is complete with descriptions of brightness and color.

2. **Identify** Identify the variables in this experiment. List them below.

_____

_____

Conclude

1. **Interpret** Answer the question in the problem. Compare your results with your hypothesis.

   _____

   _____

   _____

   _____

2. **Analyze** How does distance affect your perception of the brightness of an object?

   _____

   _____

   _____

3. **Apply** Judging by the results of the investigation, would you expect a red star or a yellow star to be hotter? Explain why.

   _____

   _____

   _____

CHAPTER
22 | ADDITIONAL INVESTIGATION
Distance and Brightness

OVERVIEW AND PURPOSE

You have learned that the amount of light given off by a star and the star's distance from Earth determine how bright the star appears to an observer on Earth. In this investigation, you will

- determine how distance affects the apparent brightness of a model star
- describe the relationship between apparent brightness and distance

Problem

How does distance affect apparent brightness?

Hypothesis

Think about what you know about stars. Use this information to write a hypothesis to suggest how the apparent brightness of a star is related to the star's distance from Earth. Write your hypothesis as an "If . . . , then . . . , because . . ." statement.

_____

_____

_____

MATERIALS
- meter stick
- light meter
- masking tape
- extension cord
- 25-watt, clear light bulb in a socket

TIME
45 minutes

CHAPTER 22
Stars, Galaxies, and the Universe

Procedure

❶ Use the masking tape to secure the meter stick to a desk top or the floor. Make sure the meter stick is parallel to the edge of the desk or a wall.

❷ Place the socket at the zero end of the meter stick, as shown.

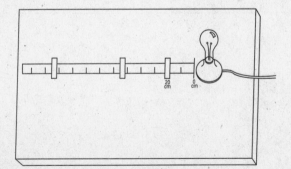

❸ Use the masking tape to secure the light cord to the desk top or the floor.

CAUTION: When you conduct this investigation, the room will be darkened. Use care when moving around the room.

④ Set the ASA of the light meter to 50.

⑤ Plug in the light bulb. Darken the room.

⑥ Hold the light meter parallel to the meter stick and measure the intensity of the light bulb at the 20-cm mark of the meter stick. Record this measurement in Table 1.

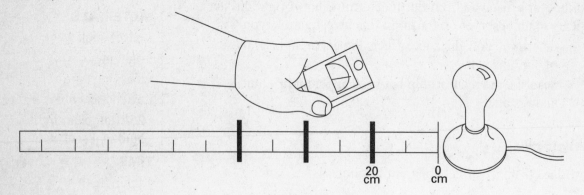

⑦ Repeat step 6, but change the distance from the light by 20 cm each time you measure light intensity until you reach 100 cm. Record your measurements in Table 1.

TABLE 1. DISTANCE VS. BRIGHTNESS

Distance from Light Bulb (cm)	Light Meter Reading (luxes)
20	
40	
60	
80	
100	

Plot your data on the graph on the next page. Plot distance from the light bulb, in centimeters, on the *x*-axis and brightness (light meter reading), in luxes, on the *y*-axis. Connect the data points with a smooth line. Give your graph a title.

Observe and Analyze

1. Analyzing Data Where was intensity the highest? the lowest?

_____

_____

_____

2. Describe Use your graph to describe how brightness changes with distance from the light bulb.

_____

_____

_____

3. Making Analogies What do the light bulb and the light meter used in this investigation represent?

_____

_____

_____

Conclude

1. **Conclude** Why does light intensity change as it does with increasing distance between the observer and the light source?

_____

_____

_____

2. **Apply** Use your results from this investigation to infer what would happen if the Sun were closer to Earth.

_____

_____

_____